The Bridge to Take When Things Get Serious

a memoir

Lori Jakiela

The Bridge to Take When Things Get Serious

a memoir

Lori Jakiela

Second Edition

CATALOGUING PUBLICATION DATA
Jakiela, Lori
Memoir, Prose.
ISBN: 069241228X; ISBN 13 9780692412282

WPA Press
Pittsburgh, Pennsylvania
www.wpapress.org

Book Layout & Design: WPA Press
Author photo credit: Heather Mull
Cover painting: Lou Ickes

Acknowledgements

Thanks to the editors of the following publications where excerpts from this book first appeared: *Atticus Review; Brevity; Fourth River; KGB BarLit: The New Yinzer; The Pittsburgh Post-Gazette; The Pittsburgh Tribune Review; Pittsburgh Quarterly; River Teeth; Superstition Review; Waccamaw Review;* and *The Washington Post.* Thank you to Laurie Abkemeier for her early edits and insights. Thank you to the late Edith Hughes, a journalist's journalist and editor's editor. Thank you to my students. You remind me every day why writing and writers matter. Thank you to my kind and talented friends and colleagues in the Pittsburgh writing and arts community, especially Scott Silsbe, Paulette Poulett, Lou Ickes, Bob Pajich, Jason Baldinger, Amy Urban, Adam Matcho, Jane Bernstein, Jane McCafferty, Jim Daniels, Karen Lillis, Paula Bohince, Emily Rodgers, Erik Cirelli, Lori Matcho, and Lesley Rains. Thank you Ed Ochester for showing me the way. Thank you Judith Vollmer for all the years. Thank you to Paula Leuzzi for being there when no one else would be. Thank you to Eric Patberg for being here now. Thank you to my parents, who I will never stop missing. And thanks and love most of all to my family – Locklin, Phelan and Dave Newman – for this beautiful life.

For Newman, always, all ways

Prologue

When I asked my mother why she dyed her hair, she said, "I don't want you to be embarrassed. I don't want people to say you have an old woman for a mother."

"Won't you be embarrassed?" my mother said the day she volunteered at my high school. She said the same thing decades later when I asked her to be my date for a faculty dinner. "I'm not smart, you know."

My mother was smart. She was beautiful. It never occurred to me, no matter what, to be embarrassed of her.

If I'd understood sooner, I like to think I would have tried to help. I like to think I would have told my mother all the good things she didn't know about herself.

"Don't let anyone see me like this," my mother said when she was very sick. But I let people come.

I wanted her to know she was loved.

Chapter 1

Gina pulls up in her black Volkswagen, reaches across and gives the passenger side door a shove. "You look like crap," Gina says. "Sally will know what to do."

Sally is Gina's psychic. Gina is taking me to see Sally as a welcome-home gift. Gina thinks this is a good idea. I do not, but because Gina means well, I try to be open.

A trio of Virgins dangles from Gina's rearview mirror like a tiny ballet troupe, their feet pirouetting on snakes. A blue statue of Mary bobs on the dash. Around Gina's neck there's another small Virgin, a St. Christopher medal, a red Italian horn. The whole car smells like vanilla air freshener and peppermint gum. New Age music clinks around on the stereo. The music sounds like coins being dropped by handfuls into a metal sink. It's meant to be soothing, like rain maybe, but it isn't.

I buckle up and check my face in the visor mirror. Gina's right. I look like crap. I look like someone who hasn't been sleeping. I haven't been sleeping. A few days before, I fell face down on the sidewalk. I had not been drinking. I had not been dizzy. I had not tripped on any discernible thing, but I'd somehow gone down beneath a sign for Jesters Tattoo Shop. Jesters' logo is a laughing devil in a flaming jingle bell cap. There is still gravel in my chin. My right hand is scabbed over. My right shoulder aches.

Gina flicks her mirrored sunglasses onto her head, slaps the visor up, and says, "You won't be sorry."

Ever since I moved back to Pittsburgh, I've been a wreck. My father is dead, and my mother is heartbroken and sick. She has breast cancer. It's in remission, but now her heart, the actual organ, is failing.

"A bee's nest," the doctor says. The list of possibilities is long, awful – heart attack, stroke, embolisms. "It's hard to say what will happen," the doctor says. "We'll do what we can."

"Do what you have to do," my mother said when I asked if she wanted me to come home. "We're fine."

After 50 years of marriage, my mother can't give my father up. His death is unthinkable, impossible to translate. When I try to imagine how my mother feels, I turn to words I'd never use for anything else, as if only something as logical as science could hold such sadness. Symbiotic, symbiosis. A molecular, cellular loss.

"It's freezing out," she said the day he died. It was snowing. The wind felt like a slap. My mother tried to stop the funeral director from lowering my father's bronze casket into the ground, like she was worried my father would die out there. "We can't bear it," she'd said, meaning the cold.

We.

There was no we. My mother was alone. She couldn't remember how to write a check. There were so many pills to take. Some days she didn't get dressed.

"We do what we can," she said.

My mother needed me, though she would never use that word, need. And so I came. I left my flight attendant job in New York. Flying isn't like working for an ordinary company. The airline gave me a two-year leave. "You go take care of things at home," my supervisor said. "We'll be here when you get back."

I left my tiny rent-controlled apartment in Queens. I left a man I'd been seeing for years. He and I hadn't liked each other much, but it was something. I thought of this move back home as temporary, just until my mother got better, just until things settled down.

That's what I still tell my old boyfriend when he calls. When he's drinking or lonely, he thinks he wants me to come back.

"When?" he says, and I say, "Soon." It's an easy lie because sometimes, when I'm lonely or drinking, I want to wish it true.

The first thing my mother said to me the day I moved home was, "Well, it took you long enough." She said, "What did you have to do that was so important?" She ran her fingers through my short blonde airline-regulation bob and said, "You always did look better with hair."

Then I saw the way her fingers shook when she held a pen, the way her breathing sounded like static when she fell asleep in a chair, and I knew.

When she'd wake, at first she wouldn't recognize me, then she would. She'd say, "Oh, you're home," like I'd never been gone long, like all this time I'd been out for milk and a newspaper, like all this time she'd been here, waiting.

<>

Sally the Psychic lives in Butler, Pennsylvania. Butler is not the kind of place you'd expect to find a psychic. Butler is the kind of place where you'd expect to find cows. Tractors and slag heaps. You can get great cabbage in Butler. The whole area is pretty, if you don't mind the smell of manure. There's a lot of patchwork farmland to ogle, and I bet somewhere, in some little diner run by an old woman in fuzzy slippers and a housecoat, you can get a great slice of pie. I just can't figure out who, other than Gina, would travel miles of back roads paved with corn to get advice from someone who, in her off hours, sells cat paraphernalia at a store called The Country Kitty.

"Sally's an expert," Gina says. "Womb-regression therapy. She can take you back before you were born. You can see where things went wrong."

An ambulance races past as Gina turns towards the Turnpike and Butler. My breath catches. Every time I see an ambulance, I'm sure it's my mother. "It happens all the time," the funeral director said after my father's wake. "One goes, then the other."

Whatever our problems, my mother has always made it clear she loves me. And I love her, desperately, in the way that daughters with fierce mothers often do. I can't separate my life from hers.

"When you lose your mother," a friend told me, "you have to re-make yourself."

I can't understand this. I never want to understand this.

An hour later, we pull up to Sally's house. There's a sign nailed over the porch. It looks like something a kid made in woodshop, ragged letters burned into a piece of driftwood. The sign says Psychic Spiritual Counselor. It says, Walk-Ins Welcome. There are no neighbors.

Sally hears us pull up and comes out. I've only seen city psychics before. They always dress the part – lots of heavy jewelry, maybe a bandana. Sally wears cut-offs, tank top, and a pair of old boat shoes. Her long blonde hair frizzes in the humidity. She is tan and pretty and completely un-psychic-looking.

"I'm so glad you made it. Gina, honey, my computer's acting crazy. Maybe you can take a look? It keeps flashing on and off. Like it's possessed," Sally says and giggles. She waves her tiny ring-less hands next to her face, possessed jazz hands. Then she turns to me.

"I'm so sorry. Let's go in and have some tea," Sally says. "Gina honey, I hope you can get that old computer up and running. You're good with those things. You have a gift. I've got my life in that computer. I mean, my life. Everything."

Someone with psychic abilities should have the foresight to back-up her computer files, but I don't say so.

The kitchen is filled with copper pots and dried herbs. On the counter and sill, there are ceramic cats. The cats are playful – one with a ball of yarn, one tipping over a little carton of milk. On the refrigerator, there is a large star-shaped magnet with a message in glitter: "Psychic Spiritual Adviser to the Stars."

"We'll just settle in," Sally says. "Then we'll see what we can see. Do you want sugar? I'm not supposed to have sugar. Screws up my perception. Caffeine, too. But I love it. Sugar and caffeine. My two main food groups."

When Sally laughs, she makes a little yapping sound, like a puppy that needs to pee. She finishes with the tea tray and we go back to the computer room. Other than the computer, a card table, and one folding chair, there isn't any furniture. There are a few pillows on the floor. Sally and I sit on these. Gina tinkers with the computer until Sally's screensaver, a picture of lions in the wild, stops flashing. Gina fiddles some more, then hits the volume button. A tin version of the theme from "Born Free" cracks and chirps.

"You are a genius!" Sally says. "I've been saved!" She begins singing.

I am glad for Sally, glad her computer has not eaten her life like a nit. But she's brought a deck of tarot cards on the tea tray and I'm waiting for her to pick them up. She doesn't. She and Gina make computer small talk instead. I try to drink my tea. It's herbal. It tastes like licorice and pond scum. It tastes medicinal, like something my mother might have forced on me as a child. "Just hold your nose and drink," she'd say and push the cup to my lips. "You want to get better? You have to help yourself."

A few moments later, mid-sentence, Sally stops talking. She looks at me and says, "Well then." She eyeballs me in a way that feels probing and intense and psychic-like. She says, "Close your eyes," and I do, even though I've always hated closing my eyes in front of other people, the vulnerability of that.

"Relax," Sally says. Now that I can't see, her voice seems different, deeper, steadier.

"Breathe," Sally says, and I breathe, deep and full, a good patient.

I know now what I want, why I'd agreed to this. I want a diagnosis and a cure, whatever way it comes. Gina has her dashboard virgins, her medals, her New Age hope. The priest at my father's funeral held my hand. He said, "Pray with me." But I couldn't. I couldn't open my mouth.

"In. And out," Sally says.

I feel myself float. My lungs fill and roll like waves.

Soon Sally will tell me that Armand, my spirit guide, says I should take vitamins and get my eyes checked. She'll say I should take up painting and possibly ceramics.

Mid-session, she'll pull her hair and break down weeping over her own failed marriage, her rotten husband who's taken most of the furniture and sent her business belly-up.

"Never trust a Leo," she'll say between sobs.

But in these first few moments, with only the sound of her voice and my breathing, Sally gives me something and I'm grateful.

"I want you to visualize," Sally says. "Let the images come."

For what seems like a long while, there's nothing. And then there is a face.

It's an old man I'd seen the day I'd fallen in front of the tattoo shop. He seemed drunk, like he just left a bar, but he didn't stagger. His steps were careful and sure. He was dressed in work clothes, the way my father had dressed – a faded blue shirt and worn jeans, steel-toed boots, a handkerchief in his side pocket. He may have just been getting off night trick. He may have stopped for a few beers before heading home.

"Ah sweetheart," the man said. "Took a dive now?"

I expected him to help me up. Instead, he stepped around me and kept going.

"Don't worry, sweetheart," he said. "We've all been there."

Chapter 2

I am my mother's caregiver. I am a 34-year-old woman who sleeps in her childhood bedroom with a Donald Duck nightlight and a mother who tries to regulate her bedtime.

"Are you going to stay up all night reading?" my mother says. "Are you going to burn that light all night long?"

"What's so important in that book you can't put it down?" my mother says. "You're going to ruin your eyes if you don't stop already."

I have seen the doctor's reports, her medical records. I know how sick she is. But some days she doesn't seem sick at all. She seems angry.

I think I know what she wants.

"Are you going to stay in that bathtub all night?" she says, pounding on the bathroom door.

"Why don't you eat meatloaf?" she says. "You think you're too good for meatloaf?"

My mother wants her heart strong.

She wants her brain clear.

She wants her husband alive in his place at the kitchen table, next to her in bed.

She wants order.

She wants her world to right itself.

<>

I take an apartment near my mother's house, but I never stay in it. There's no furniture there, no groceries. It's more of a life raft than an actual place to live.

"It's always something with you," my mother says.

My mother's house is in the suburbs, but wilderness is everywhere, which means snakes but other things, too.

"I wish I had a gun," my mother says when she looks out her bedroom window to find deer in her vegetable garden. She makes an imaginary gun, thumb and forefinger. She pulls the trigger and says *pow.*

There are squirrels and groundhogs and moles and rabbits. There are hawks and field mice, woodpeckers and bats and owls. And there are raccoons.

One night shortly after I moved home, there was a sound outside. It was furious and feral, a growl, then a snarl, then a crash of metal and breaking glass. It was more terrifying than anything I'd heard during my years in New York City, where sirens seemed like birdsong. It was more terrifying than my Queens neighbor Rocco and the chain saw he'd rev up to cut scrap metal at midnight.

"Raccoons, those rabid bastards," my mother said the next morning. There was trash all over the yard. Broken bottles glittered on the neighbor's porch. Mangled balls of aluminum foil and chicken bones and rotted hunks of meatloaf littered the driveway.

My mother said, "Get me the magnet."

"What?" I said.

"The magnet," she said. "Off the fridge. Just do it."

On my mother's refrigerator, there's a magnet shaped like a van. Cartoon critters poke their heads out of the van's windows. A raccoon is driving. The magnet says *Critter Control.* The phone number is 1-800-CRITTER. My mother is a regular. The company relocates problem animals. They set traps to help unhappy homeowners catch everything from rattlesnakes to pigeons. When the animal in question gets caught in a trap, Critter Control relocates it somewhere wild and safe and far away.

"I am not putting up with this," my mother said. "Go through my garbage and make a mess in my yard? We'll see about that."

The Critter Control guy was nice. He was professional. He dressed like a postal worker and had teeth like Scrabble tiles.

"Don't worry, ma'am," he told my mother. "We always get them."

When he smiled his mouth looked like a trap.

"You have a great day," he said. "Call us when you get a full one."

My mother glowed like a schoolgirl.

<>

"Good Morning to You," my mother sings every morning at 8 a.m. The tune is Happy Birthday. Her voice is weak, but persistent. She's always been tone deaf and no one, not even my father the singer, ever told her. It's like waking up to Rocco's chainsaw. It's like waking up to a pack of raccoons gone wild for meatloaf.

My mother follows the good morning song by snapping open the shade and yanking the covers off my bed. She did this for the first 18 years of my life. She does it now.

"You've never been a morning person," she says.

"Don't sleep your life away. There's a whole wild world out there."

She means wide world.

She means get up already.

<>

A few months back, I got a job teaching writing at a local college. Today I go off to teach my morning classes and leave my mother alone for a few hours.

"Rest," I say. "Don't do anything. I'll be back soon."

"I'm not an invalid," she says. "You live your life, I'll live mine."

And now this.

My mother is in the driveway in her robe and running shoes. Her hair is in pin curls. She wears pantyhose under her robe and, as far as I can tell, nothing else.

It's noon. It's Spring. The sun shines, the birds sing. My mother has a shovel. She holds it over her head. Beneath the loose flesh, the muscles in her arms are sinewy, tight as guitar strings.

"Jesus Mary and Joseph," she screams. "Bitch and bastard."

She pumps the shovel up and down. She stomps her feet. She looks like a straggler from an angry mob.

"What are you doing?" I say. "Would you please tell me what you're doing?"

She points. Her chest heaves. "Snake," she says between breaths. "A goddamn snake."

The snake is frantic. Part of its tail is yellow and squashed flat. This makes it stick to the driveway. I've never seen a snake limp. It's sad the way it tries to squiggle and jerk free.

I feel sorry for this one, right until it works up momentum, unglues its tail, and heads straight for me. Then I do what any responsible adult caregiver of an aging, unwell and possibly deranged parent would do. I scream, dart toward the garage, and hide behind my mother.

"It's o.k.," she says. "I've got it."

From where I crouch behind my mother's right shoulder, I try to evaluate things. The snake is small. My mother is worked up. The shovel is heavy. Killing snakes is not on her doctor's Heart-Safe Approved Activities list.

"Let it go," I say. "It's just a garter snake."

"Garter snake my ass," my mother says. She swats the air with the shovel. "That's a copperhead."

When I was six, my mother and I went blackberry picking in the woods around the house. We ran into a copperhead wrapped around the base of a blackberry bush. The head was large, heart-shaped, penny-colored. The snake seemed huge, as most things from childhood do. It seemed thick as my father's arm.

My mother -- calm, invincible -- eased my hand out of the bush and held a finger to her lips. "If you don't bother it, it won't bother you," she said.

But now things are different. The world is a more dangerous place.

"Let it go," my mother says, "and the next thing you know it's in the house. You want to wake up with that thing in bed with you?"

I'm already having trouble sleeping. Most nights I lie awake and listen to my mother breathe in the next room. Whenever there's a pause, a space between snores, I get up to check.

"What the hell are you doing?" she said the other night when she woke to find my face close to hers, my fingers under her nose checking for air.

I want to keep my mother safe. I don't know how to do this, and so I do what I watched my father do for years. I check the locks on the doors and windows. I check the gas on the stove. I check the smoke detectors, wait for the tiny green lights to flash. I watch from the doorway for my mother's chest to rise and fall.

When I do sleep, I have bad dreams, even though the bed is familiar, even though the lumps are exactly where I wore them down decades ago. I dream of my father, the way he looked before he died, the birdlike bones in his feet and hands. I wake up sweating in a room that hasn't changed since I was a child – the same raspberry shag carpet, the same pink afghan,
the same dresser with the same cracked mirror. It takes me a few minutes to know where I am and why.

I am in my mother's house. I am here to take care of her.

I am, and always will be, her child.

<>

Back in the driveway, my mother stands with her legs apart, the shovel held high. She looks completely in and out of control at once.

"That's no copperhead," I say. The snake is gimping now, headed for the road that separates our house from the woods.

My mother sprints forward. She whacks the snake again and again. The shovel clangs against the asphalt and the snake spins, coils, tries to strike. It has the kind of confidence that must be backed by venom.

"I told you! I told you!" my mother screams.

She jumps back and brings the shovel down again, this time on the snake's lispy skull.

My mother has never looked stronger or more determined in her life.

"Not in my house," she says as she pounds the snake flat. "Not in my house."

Chapter 3

That apartment I mentioned – it's on Pittsburgh's South Side, Carson Street, the main drag, a few blocks from Jester's Tattoos and its tricky sidewalk. The apartment is a train-car walk-up with crooked floors and bad plumbing. The landlord is a tiny red-faced woman built like a toaster who told me upfront she has a policy against renting to women.

"Women are hell on the plumbing," she told me the day I signed my lease. "With their periods and all."

She paused, sized me up. Her head was level with my shoulders, but her up-do made her seem taller. "I'm making an exception here, considering your mother and all." She rolled her shoulders back, posturing, and inspected the lease twice, even though she'd watched me sign it. "Your mother sounds like a nice woman," she said. "You don't use tampons, do you?"

My next-door neighbor Simon pays half what I do in rent. He does not use tampons. The landlord likes him. She thinks he's cute. He's small, like her, but with viney black hair and eyes like grapes, perfect because Simon is the sommelier at Le Pommier, an overpriced pseudo-French restaurant five blocks down.

"*Je ne sais quoi*," Simon says to explain away his charm.

About the landlord, he says, "She does have a point about the plumbing."

My first-floor neighbor, George, is a Grateful Dead fan home on workman's comp. I think he pays less than I do, too. George says he picked up Lyme Disease while climbing Machu Picchu.

"No one knows how I suffer," George told me in tears when I first met him.

It's what my grandmother used to say about her arthritic knees. It's what my father said before he got so sick he couldn't talk any more. It's a strange thing to hear from a chubby young man in a tie-dye t-shirt.

The whole building smells like George's strawberry incense and dry rot, but even my woman-rent is manageable -- $350 a month, including utilities.

When I lived in New York, I used to dream that if I opened my closet door wider, I'd find a secret passage to another room, maybe two, which would explain why my rent was $1200 for a studio the size of a walk-in freezer. This, I've learned, is a dream many New Yorkers have. Living in New York makes a person value things like space and solitude and roach-free toothbrushes. Living with my mother makes me value things, too.

"Normal people don't stay up all hours," my mother says. "Why can't you go to bed like the rest of us?"

This apartment is a luxury I can barely afford.

"I won't be living here full time," I told the landlord. "It's more for emergencies."

"That's a relief," she said, and didn't ask what I meant by emergencies.

<>

There are four rooms – living room, kitchen, bedroom, office – all lined up like dominoes. The space feels huge. Sometimes, when my mother's having a good day, when I have time off, I come here and just walk from room to room, feeling it.

I store things here – books, mostly. Some towels. I keep a bottle of wine in the fridge. There's one wine glass, a couple cups and bowls, a handful of silverware. I don't own any real furniture. Gina loaned me an air mattress I can blow up with a hair dryer. "Just in case," she said, but the one time I tried to blow it up, it leaked.

When the answering machine in the kitchen blinks, it's either a wrong number or a drunk-dialed call from New York. My old boyfriend, Gina and my mother are the only people who have this number. Gina and my mother always know where I am. My old boyfriend does not.

"Where've you been?" he says. "Call back." It's an order, a way of half-communicating he picked up in the Army. His accent is thicker than I remember. Already I have to look at pictures to remember how handsome he is, or to remember the scars that cover his chest, burns from scalded milk when he was a child. The scars are raised, a relief map. His chest is hairless, thickly muscled. He says he could stab himself with needles right there, over his heart, and he wouldn't feel it.

When my father was dying, my boyfriend stayed in New York. He didn't come to the funeral. He didn't send flowers. He couldn't understand why I didn't come right back. "It wasn't like you weren't expecting it," he said of my father's death.

People stay together for years without loving each other because loneliness is worse.

Lately, when I see the red light flashing, I erase the message without listening.

<>

I don't ever sleep at the apartment. If I did I'm sure I could fall asleep to the sounds of traffic and drunks, car alarms and police sirens. It's like New York, the comforting static of the city, but better because this is Pittsburgh and Pittsburgh is home. I've always loved cities, but I loved this city first.

As a girl, I'd hop a bus and take it into Pittsburgh. My mother would worry, but she'd let me go. A little freedom developed character, she thought, so sometimes she forced herself to say yes.

The bus stopped and picked up at the McDonald's on Forbes. I knew my way to the Point, to that place where three rivers came together. I knew the fountain. I loved to sit there and watch the incline wobble up Mt. Washington. The incline is red and black. It looked, still looks, like a ladybug.

I don't remember hold old I was for those first bus trips, but I must have been very young because the mills were still going. I'd come home and the collar of my shirt would be filthy. I'd blow my nose, and the tissue would go black with steel dust.

"Jesus, Mary and Joseph," my mother would say.

It didn't matter.

From one window of the South Side apartment I can see the Grant Building. Thirty-three stories. The lights on top of the building are a flashing beacon. They're supposed to spell out Pittsburgh in Morse Code, but as a girl I thought they spelled "I love you." The lights are red, like a lit cigarette. They look like a beating heart. A while back, a retired pilot translated the lights and found that they really spelled out Pitetsbkrrh. Maybe this way, the wrong way, is prettier.

Along Carson Street there are coffee shops where sad tattooed teenagers sit and play Scrabble all day. There's Dee's Bar, where the bartenders are all older women who pull their gray hair back in ponytails or wear wife-beater shirts to show off their muscular arms. They're good at what they do, don't tolerate rowdy drunks, barely tolerate the hipsters that come in on weekends.

Once when I was at the bar a young guy came in. The kid was pierced everywhere, his lips, his eyebrow. He had a big silver stud in his chin where a dimple should be.

"What will you have?" the bartender asked. "My usual," the kid said. His smile was a smirk, a swoosh. "Honey," the bartender said, "I don't know your usual."

When she poured, the veins along her arms popped like the mountains all around this place.

There's a rickety deck off the back of the apartment where I could sit and see all the houses wedged into those mountains. Pittsburghers call that part of the city The Slopes. Like many things here, it's an understatement. The streets going up to those houses are so vertical it feels as if a car would tumble off backwards. During bad snows, people get trapped on The Slopes and can't come down. Snow plows can't get up. At night, no matter the season, The Slopes are so dark it looks like the houses are suspended mid-air, constellations of porch lights.

"The Paris of Appalachia," the great writer Chuck Kinder calls Pittsburgh.

Chapter 4

Today, back at my mother's house, Aunt Thelma is coming over for lunch. Thelma is bringing Kentucky Fried Chicken.

"I'm not an invalid," my mother says when I suggest salad. "I'm not a rabbit. I can eat what I want."

"At least peel off the skin," I say.

"The skin," my mother says, smiling. "That's the best part."

When Thelma shows up with a bucket under her arm and her red lipstick on, I drive to the apartment. I roll the window down and enjoy the quiet, the feel of the wind and sun. I try not to think about my mother.

I find a lucky parking space out front. It's the one space without a meter, but it's legal. George let me in on it. George is nice and harmless, but I suspect he's never been to Machu Picchu and that he's not really sick.

"This Lyme Disease is tricky. Those doctors can't tell," George always says.

I try to be quiet on the stairs. I try to be quiet when I pass George's apartment. His stereo is on. Jerry Garcia wails. The hallway smells like a church. I think I've almost made it when the door pops open and there's George, in swim trunks, a towel wrapped around his head.

"Hey there, neighbor," he shouts over the smoke and music. "I've got something for you."

George waves me inside his apartment. I don't want to go, and so I stand in the doorway and smile. I brace my hand on the doorframe.

"I'm only popping in," I say. "A quick mail check."

"It will only take a second," George says, but when he sees I'm not following, he holds up one finger, then walks into the next room. I hear him fumbling with something. It sounds heavy. Something else crashes, then more fumbling. Soon he's back, pushing an orange wing-backed chair.

"You want this?" George says, out of breath now, his towel-turban drooping over one eye. "I'm downsizing. Clearing my karma and that. It's not all that comfortable. But you can have it if you want."

The chair is crushed velvet. The orange is the color of muddy soda pop. It has claws for legs. But it's sturdy, a real piece of furniture. I imagine the chair, sitting in it.

Of course I want it.

George doesn't help me get the chair up the next two flights of stairs. "This Lyme Disease," he says. "No one knows." But I drag it up and wedge it through the door and it feels like a step toward something.

I pull the chair through the living room, through the kitchen, and out the sliding glass door. The deck is wood, rotting. Like the floors in the apartment, like the roof, like George's towel-turban, the deck slants, leans. It's probably dangerous. Off in the distance, the houses on the slopes are all colors and sizes. They look glued on, a collage.

"What kind of people build houses on the sides of mountains?" John Edgar Wideman, a Pittsburgh-born writer, asked once.

People who have no respect for gravity. People who have a lot of faith. People who believe the world won't turn on them, that everything they've built their lives around won't collapse.

I go inside and pour a glass of wine. It's the kind of wine that would make Simon, the wine expert, wince.

"Oh that's good," he'd say, "on salad."

Back outside on the deck, I sit in the chair and cradle the glass in my hand. The wine is cold and clean. I feel almost happy -- happy to have this chair, this place, a little quiet to come to.

Happy to be alone, happy to stare out at the lights in all those houses and not think.

Chapter 5

My mother and Thelma decide to make their lunch date a regular thing.

"She needs some normalcy," Thelma says.

"I'm thinking Hoss's," my mother says. "A nice big steak."

Thelma brought my mother a stack of joke books and they take turns reading from them. "Laughter is the best medicine," Thelma says gravely, as if she just now thought of it.

Free for the afternoon, I drive back to the apartment. The weather is warmer and, if I'm going to be spending more time here, I'll need to get a room air conditioner to make it live-able.

I tip-toe past George's door and try not to cough. He's kicked the incense up, maybe switched scents, maybe patchouli. His music is turned up loud, as usual, and someone, George I'm sure, sings along, off key.

When I open the door to the apartment, the smell is like a slap. It smells like cat litter. It smells like a frat house. It smells like bleach and broccoli and New York in summer, by which I mean the subway, by which I mean it smells like piss.

I move through the apartment and try to find the source. A cat might have gotten in. I check the windows to see if they're shut. I check the carpet for wet spots. But when I get to the kitchen, it's clear.

The chair sits where I left it. I'd brought it off the deck in case it rained. It's here in the center of the kitchen, its clawed feet and arm rests sprawled, regal, a throne.

I bend down and sniff to be sure. The smell clears my sinuses.

Someone, most likely George, has peed on this chair.

George, that lunatic, who is downstairs wailing out the chorus of The Grateful Dead's "Truckin'" and getting stoned on jelly-scented incense, has given me, as a gift, as an act of neighborly generosity, a pee chair.

"Beware a gift horse's mouth," my mother, master of the mixed metaphor, would say.

I feel like crying.

Still, it's the only furniture I have. I walk downstairs and to the grocery store across the street. I buy upholstery cleaner and Lysol. I trudge back up, this time not even bothering to be stealthy. I stomp, furious, duped. I think George knows, because even if he hears me, he doesn't, for once, come out.

Back in the apartment, I drench the chair with cleaner. I scrub it down with Lysol. I soak the cushions until I'm choking from the fumes.

There's a knock on the door, then the sound of the door opening. I expect George, his big head bobbing like a buoy and full of shame, but it's Simon carrying a copy of Camus' *The Stranger* and a stack of junk mail.

"Your mailbox was overflowing again, so I thought I'd be a boy scout," he says. He plops the mail on the counter, then sniffs. He holds up Camus like a fan and starts flapping. "Dear Lord. You didn't clog the plumbing, did you?"

Beaten, useless, I point at the chair. Simon shrugs but doesn't ask. Instead, he says, "Have you read Camus?" He pronounces it Cam-us, the S, one long hiss, and I say, "No."

I first read Camus back in college. I loved how he could believe and not believe all at once. I loved the way he struggled to balance hopelessness and hope. We die, Camus said, which means life is meaningless. We live, Camus said, and find meaning and beauty there.

After Simon finally leaves, I sit on the kitchen floor and stare at the chair. To take it to the trash, I'll have to walk past George's apartment. He knows he's given me a pee chair, but twisted as it seems, I'd feel ungrateful ditching it. I could wait until George is out of town but George never goes out of town. George rarely leaves his apartment.

The goal of all art is to gain access to the one or two images that first gained access to our hearts.

Camus said that, too.

Here are two images -- a woman on her knees in a nearly empty room; an orange chair she's covered, like a body, with a sheet.

Chapter 6

In the morning, I'm not a good teacher. I'm cranky. My students are hung-over or asleep. Wednesdays are the worst. I start at 8:30 a.m. and don't finish until 10 p.m.

"How's the teaching going?" my mother asks.

I've heard her on the phone to the neighbors. "My daughter, the professor," she says. It sounds impressive. It's not. I work at a branch campus. I make slightly more money than I did as a flight attendant. My university office is in the basement next to the boiler room. The dean gives junior faculty like me a cruel mix of early morning and night classes because he believes it builds character.

"He'll make exceptions if you sleep with him," a senior faculty member told me.

The dean jogs around campus in red booty shorts. He dyes his hair the color of wet asphalt. There's often hair dye smudged around his forehead, on the tips of his ears. His forehead is square and high. His teeth are capped and shiny, like they're slicked with Vaseline.

A few days ago, he cornered me with his idea of a serious academic question. "Are you a new woman?" he asked. "Or an old woman?" Then he winked and walked away.

"Teaching's good," I tell my mother. "I'm happy to be home."

I tell myself this, too. I recite it like a mantra. It's what I'm telling myself now as I down my fourth cup of coffee and try to focus. It's Wednesday, 8:45 a.m. One of my journalism students recounts an interview she's done with Mister Rogers' estranged sister Elaine.

"I think she's still angry about the whole Lady Elaine thing? You know, the puppet with the big nose with the wart on it?" Shannon says. "The really ugly one who lives in the Museum Go Round?"

Shannon's favorite color is bright orange, the kind hunters wear so they don't get shot. Shannon is very blonde. She looks lovely in orange, like the high beams on an expensive car, but it's early. Looking directly at Shannon hurts my eyes, so I study my coffee. I swish and swirl and stare as if there's something magical -- the future maybe -- in the sludge-stained bottom of my cup.

"See, the thing is, Mr. Rogers modeled Lady Elaine after her?" Shannon says. "She's still not over it?"

Everything Shannon says is a question.

Shannon is the sun asking permission to shine.

I've never thought about the characters in Mr. Rogers' Neighborhood – prissy King Friday in his petticoats; X the Owl, a fraud taking correspondence classes; scared little Henrietta Pussycat, who knew few words other than "meow." It never occurred to me that they might be based on real people.

Since Pittsburgh was Mister Rogers' real-life neighborhood, these people would likely be local. Real, local people who, when confronted with the puppet versions of themselves, wouldn't always like what they saw.

"There's only one of everybody, toots," Lady Elaine liked to say.

It's hard to imagine Mr. Rogers estranged from anyone. It's hard to imagine him ever being cruel.

"Sounds like you have a great story," I tell Shannon. "You've got news value – conflict, proximity, celebrity, human interest. Run with it."

I haven't been a reporter in a newsroom for 14 years, but I still say things like "news value" and "run with it" and "you've buried your lede." I still love the archaic smell of newsprint. I still love the idea that stories, when they're told right, can change things.

I finish my coffee and say, "O.k. Who's next?" when there's a knock on the door. The knock is loud, urgent, all bone on wood. It's Bernie. Bernie makes an eye shield with her hands and presses her face to the glass.

If Mr. Rogers knew Bernie, the faculty secretary, maybe he'd have based a puppet on her. Bernie wears astonishingly bright makeup, all pinks and purples and blues. Her clothes are tight and cinched with a belt. Her white blonde hair is usually done up in a ponytail or a twist, cheerleader style, with sparkly barrettes and bows. Bernie is in her fifties. When she was young, she'd been a cheerleader. Now she makes everything about herself perky.

But Bernie isn't perky. She's miserable. She hates her job. She hates the other secretaries. She hates liberal types, people like college professors and students. And she hates the copy machine, which is located outside my office door.

"They don't pay me enough to deal with this crapola," she told me one day after she'd kicked the machine twice and left a dent. "Just yesterday, I got toner all in my face. It spit at me. There was toner in my nose, in my hair, everything. I looked like," and here she paused, looked around and lowered her voice, the way people do when they talk about cancer, when they're about to say something they know they shouldn't even think. "A black woman."

I usually stay clear of Bernie. Now here she is, first thing in the morning, her rainbow-colored face filling the window. This can't be good, but there's nothing else to do so I wave her in.

"I thought you'd want to see this," she says and hands me a note. "I think it's an emergency. I figured I'd want to know if I were you."

The note says, "Call home. Your mother's sick."

Then Bernie does something unexpected. She squeezes my arm. It is a kind, small gesture and I'm grateful.

"We have to stop here," I tell the class. "We'll pick up next time."

Micah, a kid in the back row sleeping, jolts up, scowls, then bobs back down.

Shannon starts to say, "What are we supposed to do," but before she can finish, I'm gone.

Chapter 7

By the time I make it from campus to my mother's house, our neighbor Margie is there. Margie is a nurse, like my mother. They worked together at Braddock Hospital years ago and have been friends ever since.

Margie kneels next to my mother, who lies on the couch in the living room.

"She's being stubborn. As usual," Margie says.

Margie's hair is the color of dried blood. She tries to hold my mother's hand. My mother keeps pulling away. Margie talks loud and slow, sing-song-y, as if my mother and I don't speak English, as if we can't understand.

Margie says, "I told her 'Bert, let me call the ambulance. Let's get you out of here.' But she wouldn't have it, now would you, Bert?"

My mother flops her head deeper into the pillow.

Margie scrunches up like she's about to be hit. Margie says, quieter, "She wants you to take her."

"I don't want a fuss," my mother says. She looks pale and waxy. Sometime before all this, she'd packed a bag with her slippers, nightgown and toothpaste. She's been sick so often, she knows the routine. The bag is there, waiting where she'd put it, by the door.

"You know how the neighbors are," she says. "They see an ambulance and they stand around and gawk. I don't want everyone looking at me. I'm not an invalid. Now let's go."

But she doesn't move. She looks furious. She looks like she might cry. I sit down near her head, smooth her hair away from her face. She doesn't try to stop me, even though her hair will be standing up and a mess and she'll hate that. We stay there for what feels like too long – we should rush, get up, get going – but it's probably only seconds.

I'm starting to believe life is full of little deaths, moments that feel like the world and everything in it stops and waits and considers whether or not to go on.

Margie still talks, but she sounds as if she's floating away.

Margie is just a few years older than me. She has three great kids, left her nursing job to stay home, never forgets a birthday or anniversary, likes pipe-cleaner crafts, and dotes on my mother. During the time I'd been away from home, Margie took on the role of my mother's other daughter.

"She's the good one," my mother says, and I always check to see if she's joking. I don't think she is. Margie has always been there. I have not.

"Are you a new woman?" the dean had asked. "Or an old woman?"

Modern or old-world. Selfish or selfless. As if these were the only choices. After my father died, I tried to go back to work. I took a trip to Brussels, a 24-hour layover. I thought going back to work would be a good thing. My original plan wasn't to move home. It was to commute between Pittsburgh and my airline's base in New York. I'd fly a three-day trip, then come home to check on my mother. I was finally senior enough to hold a good schedule – three days on, three days off.

When I had to fly, I wouldn't be gone long, and I hoped it would help my mother adjust. If we acted like the world would go on, I thought, it would.

At around 3 a.m. Brussels' time, the phone rang in my hotel room. I was awake. I'd forgotten to pack the over-the-counter sleeping pills I'd been using to help me sleep and ward off jet lag. I liked the pills because they kept me from dreaming.

When the phone rang, I'd just gotten out of the bathtub. I was eating my way through a bag of mushroom-shaped truffles and watching the world news. I picked up, figuring it was the front desk or a wrong number. Instead, it was a supervisor from my airline.

"Darlin'," the voice on the phone said, a thick southern accent, the words fluffed up like a feather bed. "Your mother had a heart attack, a small one. Don't worry. She's fine. Your neighbor Margie is trying to reach you. Here's the number. You can call now. We'd get you on the first flight out, but you're already working it. Sorry, darlin'."

I called my mother's hospital room. Margie was there, and I was relieved my mother wasn't alone. But I felt something else, too, something that, as an only child, I'd never felt before. I'm not sure there's a word for it, but if there is, it would be something territorial, something awful stirred up by grief and fear.

I should have been with my mother. I needed to be there. I wasn't there. Margie was. And I hated it. I hated Margie. I hated myself. I hated that I'd chosen to keep flying, that I'd tried to go on as if everything was the way it always was. It seemed selfish, hopeless. I felt all of this, all at once, alone in this hotel where, the next morning, I'd have difficulty explaining to the French-speaking woman at the front desk that I didn't have money to pay the phone bill.

"Perhaps you should have considered this," she'd say.

When Margie picked up the phone, my voice cracked. I pulled the hotel robe tight around me.

"Don't worry," Margie said. "She's fine."

I said, "Put my mother on the phone."

"She's fine," Margie said. "She's tired."

I said, "Put her on."

There was fumbling and static, whispering, then finally, my mother's voice, drugged and weak, barely there at all.

She said, "Lori?"

She said, "Is that you?"

She said, "Where are you?"

"All of us have special ones who loved us into being," Mr. Rogers said once during a speech. He asked everyone to take ten seconds to think of these people. Ten seconds of silence. Then he looked at his watch. "Don't worry," he said. "I'll watch the time."

I look at my mother on the couch. Margie, this room, everything falls away. Here in these silent seconds, it's only my mother and me. I stroke my mother's hair, her face, and my mother, fragile and small as a child, closes her eyes and lets me.

Chapter 8

I'm afraid my mother will collapse on the way to the car, but she insists on walking without help.

"I said I'm not an invalid," she says, and looks across the street to be sure no neighbors are watching. "Bring my bag and my pillow. You know I can't sleep on those hospital pillows. They're hard as rocks."

She's cranky again, a good sign. I follow behind to make sure she doesn't fall. I help her into the car, where she pops the glove compartment and takes out a bottle of baby aspirin. She took nitroglycerine before we left and now it's kicking in. This wipes out the chest pains and replaces them with nausea and a headache.

"I hate all this crap," my mother says, and leans her head against the window.

We are both calm. We've been through this before, many times. After the first moments of crisis, everything starts to feel like a drill, like something we do in the event of an emergency.

"Business as usual," my mother says to the doctor who meets us at the emergency room. "Just be sure I don't die in here. I don't like all these white walls. They give me the creeps."

For years, three things broke up the white on my parents' walls at home -- two plastic-framed paintings and a crucifix the size of a ham.

The paintings had been on sale at Woolworth's.

"A steal," my mother said. "It's not every day you can get great art at that price."

"Stupidest damn things I've ever seen," my father said. "My dog can do better than that."

The paintings were a matched set – two big-eyed moppets dressed as harlequins. One wore pink tights, the other blue. They were sad little girls with mandolins. They had heads like buoys and jellybean feet, and their eyes were black and glossy, as if they'd lived long and seen every sorrow in the world and weren't little girls at all.

As for the crucifix, it hung over my parents' bed. It wasn't what it appeared to be, either.

It was a hollow box. Inside was a bottle of holy water, rosary beads, a vial of oil, two candles, and a prayer book. A Last Rites kit, my mother explained.

"In case the priest doesn't make it in time," she said as she dusted Jesus' nooks and crannies with a Q-tip. Jesus looked like a bronze dragonfly without wings. He seemed to be shrugging.

"It's good to be prepared," my mother said.

My father's mother died before I was born. She had a bad heart and died in her sleep while my mother sat next to her in a chair. One minute my grandmother was breathing. Then she wasn't. "I want to go like that," both my parents would say.

The Last Rites kit had been a gift. My grandmother, my mother's mother, gave it to my parents on their wedding day. She thought this was a good and practical thing. My mother had been sick since birth, and would, years later, have the distinction of being the only person in her family, the only person I knew of, period, to receive Last Rites four times. She'd had her first round when she was eight or nine – heart problems, anemia.

"They didn't know what was wrong with me," my mother said. "But they were sure I wouldn't make it through the night."

Someone called the priest, who prayed and poured oil on her forehead and consoled her parents, who'd already picked out a burial plot.

Then my mother got better.

Ten years later, she'd get a visit from a priest again – this time for tuberculosis. She picked it up during her first year of nursing school. She was in isolation. The priest came, the family wept.

My mother got better.

And so, when my parents were married, my grandmother thought the crucifix would be the perfect gift. My grandmother gave a speech at the reception. "I just want you to know," she said, and raised a glass to my father. "Enjoy her while you can. She won't live long."

My mother was anointed two more times, both in a hospital, both because of heart attacks. All of this has made her seem indestructible, even today when she refused the ambulance, even when I ran red lights and we made it to the hospital in minutes.

But my mother has a living will in her purse.

My hand shakes when I fill out her paperwork.

<>

My father died at home, in a spare bedroom that the hospice nurses had set up like a hospital room. To give my father something to look at, my mother hung a calendar on the wall.

It had pictures of teddy bears dressed in prom gowns on it. It was better than the crucifix or a blank white wall, and my father liked to count the days.

I stayed in the room with him and slept on the loveseat. I knew my father was afraid to die because he told me so, and even though I couldn't do anything about death, I didn't want him to be alone while he waited for it.

I tried not to cry in front of him, but one day, when he was very sick and moving in and out of consciousness, I couldn't help it. I thought he wouldn't notice, and so I sat in a corner of the room and wept. I didn't try to stop it. I must have been making a horrible fuss because my father woke up. He turned his head to me and his eyes seemed bright and lucid, no trace of morphine.

He looked at me and smiled and said, "Don't cry, honey. I'm not going anywhere. I'm going to be around."

I was a child again and he was my father and I believed him.

That was the last conscious thing my father said to me.

He died two weeks later.

The adult in me, the person who'd been giving my father his medications, who'd made decisions about his care and tried to buffer my mother from stress and grief, expected this. The child in me, who lay awake at night and listened to her father breathe, expected him to keep his word.

"I'm fine," my mother says as she stretches out on the gurney and waits for more blankets and a glass of ginger ale.

The heart monitor beeps and thrums, steady, sure.

Chapter 9

The orderly's name is Rich. He's come to fill the water pitcher. Rich has eyebrows like steel wool and eyes that seem to focus anywhere but here.

"My dad used to scrunch his face up all the time, just like you," I say. "You shouldn't frown so much."

"My wife tells me that too," Rich says and goes on frowning.

"When my dad died, the lines went away," I say. "His face relaxed."

"That so?" Rich says.

"My dad worried about everything," I say.

"Lots of people do," Rich says. He jiggles the ice pitcher. He's careful to look in my direction, just not at me. He aims for a spot above my head. I recognize this technique. I've used it myself, many times.

Once, a woman on the street in New York stopped me. "Can I ask you a question?" she said.

"Sure," I said.

"Shave or wax?" she said.

"What?" I said.

"Your legs, your parts," she said. "Shave or wax?"

The question seemed important.

"Shave," I said.

"I thought so," she said. "I sure as hell thought so."

The woman didn't look crazy. She wore a ponytail and a suit. She carried a briefcase and an expensive-looking umbrella.

The umbrella had a wooden duck's head for a handle. Everything about this woman was prim and pulled together, except her mind.

"Another Number 11," my friend June said when I told her the story. June is into numerology. There's a theory, she says -- if the number of letters in your name adds up to 11, you attract negative personalities. Crazy people on the bus feel inclined to talk to you. They will seek you out and tell you their panty size. They will give you details about their sex lives and bowel habits. They will tell you where they keep the remains of their childhood pets.

I'm an 11. June is an 11. Many of my closest friends are 11s. I'm not sure what this means. Maybe 11s seek each other out so we always have someone who understands why the guy in the kilt with the imaginary bagpipes finds us irresistible.

"There's one of us," June says when she sees someone cornered.

"They see us coming," she says when it's us.

For years I was on the receiving end of crazy talk. Then something happened. I blame it on age and grief and loss, but who knows. Whatever it was, things had reversed. Now I catch myself trying to make eye contact with strangers. I catch myself saying things.

"My father worried his life away," I tell Rich. "I'm trying not to be like him."

"Good for you," Rich says and plops down a few cups and straws.

<>

I spend the night in the chair in my mother's room. When Rich floats in, I try to keep things straight. I say hi and thanks.

I've been re-reading Hemingway, which is what I do whenever I'm having a bad time. I love the man, his books, his code. Grace under pressure. I've tried to live that way and thought I was good at it.

"It wouldn't hurt you to have an emotion once in a while," an old boyfriend once told me.

But now emotion seemed bent on taking me, no matter what. I want grace, but here in the hospital, with my mother scheduled for surgery the next morning, I'm afraid. I'm doing my best not to act out.

<u><></u>

The receptionist is the only other person in the room. It's 7 a.m. and she looks tired. She has a huge coffee mug that reads "Coffee. I'll sleep when I'm dead." She holds onto it with both hands.

"I sure could use some coffee," I say and feel pathetic, graceless.

She stares at her switchboard.

"That's a great mug," I say and feel worse.

She shuffles paperwork.

"Do you know where I could get some?" I ask. "Coffee?"

"Front lobby," she says, and points over her shoulder without looking at me.

"Thanks," I say, but I don't move. This is a good thing because just then the automatic doors swing open and the doctor comes out. He's in scrubs. He wears safety glasses. When he walks, he makes a rustling sound like he's wrapped up, a present in tissue paper. All the times I've been with my mother in his office, I never noticed how small he is, how delicate, like a boy. Doctors always seem tall and I'm shocked when I see them out of context, at the mall or in the grocery. In the world, with their wrinkled clothes and mussed hair, they look normal-sized and powerless like the rest of us.

Maybe it's the open space of the hospital, all this white light, but when he sits down, the doctor, this man who will either save or not save my mother, seems pale and breakable. He takes off the safety glasses. His eyes are blue, the same color as his scrubs, a color brewed in a test tube. He hands me a picture.

The paper is thin and shiny and there, in black and white, is an image of my mother's heart.

"You can see here," he says, and makes a circle with his finger. "And here. The arteries are closed off. The old stents are blocked. We need to go in and open things back up."

In the grainy image, my mother's heart looks like a satellite picture of a desert. The landscape is slashed with tunnels and roads. It looks like a dark and violent place. It reminds me of pictures generals show to reporters during a war. "Here," they say, and make circles with a pointer, "was a bridge. And now here, there is no bridge." The generals say things like "target" and "mission." They call war an operation.

"The operation won't take long," the doctor says. "It's best to do it now. Otherwise."

His finger circles a bottlenecked road, the only open artery. His finger is beautiful, long and squared off at the tip.

"You can always tell a good surgeon by his hands," my mother always says.

The doctor puts down the picture. "All it would take would be for this one to close and that would be that. Understand?"

I nod.

"So we're good?"

"Yes," I say, and he pats my leg, then shuffles back through the double doors that lead to surgery, where my mother waits.

He leaves the picture. I pick it up and look at it until it feels like a violation to go on looking. Then I fold it in half and put it in my bag.

<>

The receptionist is still busy playing solitaire on her computer. I pull out a list my mother asked me to make. It's a list of people she wants me to call – her sisters, neighbors, friends – when this is over.

I don't want to call these people. What Number 11s know: it's easier to talk to strangers because it's likely they'll never show up again. There's no follow up, no aftershock.

Here's what's left of my Hemingway code: I want to talk to someone. I have a list of people to call. I put the list away.

"I'm going for that coffee now," I announce to the receptionist, who goes on playing.

<>

At the coffee cart in the lobby, the coffee smells strong and burnt, but it's hot. I pick up a newspaper and think maybe later I'll feel like reading. Behind the cart, the wall is metal and glass and I catch my reflection. I look electric – my hair frizzed, my face shiny, my clothes wrinkled from the night before. I try to smooth my hair without being obvious. I wish I had some lipstick. It seems wrong to care what I look like and I don't want anyone to see me fuss, but I don't want to look like I'm falling apart, even if I am.

"Can I just get in here?" a voice behind me says. It sounds scabbed over, all whiskey and cigarettes.

I move over and make room for the woman, who I think may be a man. She is very tall. She has large hands, work hands, with chipped red fingernails gnawed down to nubs.

"I just need a little sugar, hon," she says. "It's been one hell of a night."

"It has," I say.

"We all look like hell, don't worry," she says. "Nothing a little coffee can't fix, right?"

Her hair falls like a wig. It's permed and sprayed and teased and an odd shade of red that seems cheerful as a valentine against her pink track suit. She pours sugar from the canister. She keeps on pouring until her coffee looks like syrup. Then she stops and holds the canister mid-air.

"Can I ask you something?" she says.

I nod.

"Do you love your mother?" she says.

The question, its precision and randomness, cuts. There is no way to explain this.

"Yes," I say. "Of course."

"My daughter," the woman says. "She doesn't know how to love. She learned that from my ex, that bastard."

"I'm sorry," I say.

She says, "I'm sorry, too," and passes me the sugar.

Chapter 10

In surgery, my mother starts to bleed. She loses a lot of blood and needs transfusions. When the doctor comes to tell me this, he's sweating.

"We couldn't do what we went in to do," he says. His surgical mask hangs like a doll's bib. His safety glasses are cocked on his head. The glasses push his hair up so it seems to stand on end. It's the way he looks – shocked, off center – that scares me most.

I try to focus on his voice, the steady stream of words. He says he has the bleeding under control. He says my mother is sedated. He says she is recovering.

"You can go back and see her," he says, "but she's pretty out of it."

Her skin is cool. My mother's hair has been gray for years, but I never noticed how gray. Against the pillow and white sheets, she looks like a face in the snow. "White out," they call it in Erie, the snow belt, when the snow comes down hard and people get lost and can't find their way home.

"She'll be o.k.," the nurse says, and I let her take my hand and lead me back to the waiting room where there is nothing else to do.

The receptionist still clicks away at Solitaire. I try to remember how to play but can't. A few more people filter in, all of them in little groups. They whisper and huddle, so I look for something to focus on to make it seem like I'm waiting for someone, like I'm not alone at all.

* * *

I settle for the huge clock on the wall. There are black slashes where the numbers should be and a red second hand. I watch the red hand make its jagged jumps and try not to think of blood or arteries or the way people always compare hearts to clocks.

I stare at the clock but can't say how many hours have passed. There are places where time loses traction. A hospital is one of them.

<>

In the winter in Erie, Pennsylvania, people often get drunk and try to walk across the lake to Canada. It's as close as most humans can get to walking on water, and the temptation to try it is huge.

Sometimes they make it. More often, they don't.

"It felt solid," some poor guy tells reporters every year. "And then the whole damn thing cracked open."

I hate snow and cold, but I lived in Erie during college and a few years out. In Erie, forecasters measure snowfall in feet, not inches. I had a coat that looked like a sleeping bag and a hat with fleece ear flaps. I wore battery-operated self-heating socks. I left the house looking like a giant lint-covered sausage. More often than not, I was freezing and miserable.

I'm thinking about this now, in the waiting room with the doors that divide me from my mother in her white bed of snow.

I'm thinking of it, Erie and snow, and the black slashes on the face of this clock, and the black ice that coated Erie's roadways.

Black ice looks safe, clear. This is what makes it dangerous.

The first time I spun out, I wasn't sure what happened. Time had been smooth, a ribbon of road, a film reel. Then it came apart. Slashed into snapshots. Here's a picture of my car going forward. Here's one of my foot on the gas. Here's the car in a fishtail. Here's the car spinning, slow and graceful, like dancing.

Here I am not fighting it.

Here is where I let go.

Chapter 11

When my mother wakes in her hospital room, the first thing she wants is a cup of ice chips. The second thing she wants is to watch the news.

"I don't care what channel," she says, and rolls ice on her tongue like a lozenge. Her tongue is pale, medicinal. Her lips are cracked open.

Usually, she hates the news. "The news makes me want to shoot myself," she always says. She prefers game shows, especially "Jeopardy." She likes to play with me because she always wins. She's great at giving her answers in the form of questions. "What is Morocco," she shouts. "Who is Buzz Aldrin." Then she beams. "See," she says. "I know some things."

Now she's quiet, propped on pillows, the TV blaring from the little walkie-talkie speaker next to her ear. There's weather, traffic, headlines. My mother slips in and out of sleep between ice chips. Her arms are covered with bruises from where needles went in. Her feet stick out from under the sheet. When I bend down to cover them, I can see the veins and bones.

"The news," she always says, "proves there's nothing right in the world."

A mountain in Morocco is one of the Pillars of Hercules.

Buzz Aldrin said, "The eagle has landed." He said, "Every human has a finite number of heartbeats. I don't intend to waste any of mine."

When my mother drifts off, I change channels, anything but the news. I look for Jeopardy, but can't find it. On the Home Shopping Channel, a crazed-looking woman in bright pink lipstick and a scarf tries to sell jewelry. "100 percent real cubic zirconia," she says. There's "Wheel of Fortune." There's a Spanish language channel, a telenovela, another accessorized woman in bright lipstick, weeping.

I turn the volume down, but leave the TV on for light, then I sleep off and on in the chair. I try not to move much. The chair is vinyl. It squeaks. If I'm not careful, the footrest will spring back into place and sound like thunder. I try to hold still and my mother holds still and we move through the night like this.

When I hear her wake, I put ice chips on her tongue and hold her head because I'm afraid she'll choke and because she's too weak to force me to stop. When the ice melts, water pools at the corner of her mouth and rolls down her chin.

Later I fall back asleep and dream of a desert.

"What is Egypt."

"Who is Cleopatra."

I'm afraid the answer to everything might be another question.

Chapter 12

The next morning, the sun slices the slatted hospital blinds. It glints off the steel bed rails and the heart monitor and I.V. poles. It takes a second for me to remember where I am. And then I panic.

My mother is up. She's half out of bed, swatting at the cords on her heart monitor. "You'd think," she's saying, "that after all these years they'd invent a hospital gown where your ass doesn't hang out."

I don't know how it's possible, but she's back, my fierce mother.

"Nurses make the worst patients and I've been both for years," she says to the little blonde candy-striper who drops off a fistful of saltines, then backs out the door.

"You can either get me up or get out," she says to Rich the orderly, who lifts her under both arms as she shuffles along in blue hospital booties and I wheel the I.V. she's nicknamed Fido into the bathroom.

"And look who it is," she says to the doctor. "Nice of you to show up."

He still seems unnerved. Today he's in a suit and carrying a clipboard, but his eyes dart the room like two birds looking for a way out. I can't blame him. My mother has dropped all pleasantries. She's usually flirty with doctors, including this one with his nice hands. Not now.

"I guess I gave you a run in there," she says and crosses her arms as well as she can around all the tubes and wires. "I guess you worked for your money this time around. So now what do you suggest we do?"

My mother's voice says this doctor is a stand-in for everyone who ever failed her. He is every doctor who ever talked down to her in nursing school. He is my father saying, "You empty bed pans for a living." He is my grandmother saying, "She won't live long."

The doctor clears his throat and flips through his clipboard. He sits down on the bed next to my mother and tries to explain things. New medications, physical therapy. He makes a pinching motion, finger and thumb, when he talks about the arteries. He says the drugs might help. Might. He doesn't show my mother a picture of her heart and I don't mention the one I have in my bag. It's enough to know things are bad and my mother, the nurse, understands how bad. She doesn't need to see it.

"So you want me to take another bushel-basket of pills," she says to the doctor. "Well this stinks."

"We're talking about quality of life," the doctor says. He explains that the new drugs will let her go on doing whatever she likes, within reason. They will, he says, let her get on with things.

"So what you're saying is I'll live until I die," my mother says.

"If you put it that way," the doctor says.

"Don't we all?" my mother says.

The doctor laughs. My mother doesn't.

"I want to go home," my mother says.

"In a few days," the doctor says.

"I'm ready now," my mother says.

"You can't be alone," the doctor says. "At least not at first."

"My daughter," my mother says, and her voice changes to something softer. She tilts her chin my way. "My daughter will be with me. She's my right arm. What would I do without her?"

I smile at the doctor. "Of course," I say.

"This one's a handful," he says.

"I'm a sweetheart," my mother says, and gives the IV pole a shove. "Very easy going."

Chapter 13

"I know she's sick," I tell Gina on the phone. "But she's really made a comeback."

I'm in the kitchen. My mother putters around in her bedroom. I keep my voice down and listen for footsteps.

"I'll be right over," Gina says. She's been working a lot, traveling between Pittsburgh and a ratty hotel room in Columbus, Ohio. Gina's own mother thinks Gina's job is a sham. She thinks it's an excuse for Gina to not get married and not come home.

"Cut the charades," Gina's mom tells her. "What's so special about this life of yours? I need you here. Don't turn your back on me."

I tell Gina, "You're a good woman," and Gina, who's taken to carrying Virgin Mary prayer cards in her wallet and passing them to strangers, says, "Yeah, I'm a saint."

An hour later, Gina shows up at my mother's door with seafood. Gina has stopped by Wholey's in Pittsburgh's Strip District. Wholey's is one of the few places in Pittsburgh where you can order a live fish from a tank and watch while a butcher whacks it over the head with a mallet, then skins it fresh. It seems awful and cruel and people line up to watch. Wholey's slogan is "Where the fish is so fresh, some of it's still swimming."

"Hiya Bert," Gina says to my mother and smiles. Whenever Gina smiles, she looks like a kid trying to hide a wad of gum under her tongue. She looks like she's trying to not get caught being happy. "I thought I'd come over and cook you a decent meal."

My mother is in a sweatshirt. The sweatshirt is covered with dancing teddy bears. My mother loves teddy bears. Years ago, she went through a phase where she made homemade teddy bears to sell at flea markets. She bought rolls and rolls of fake fur from the fabric store. She stuffed the bears with old pantyhose and made each one its own nametag.

The bears were beautiful, but expensive and time-consuming to make. They didn't sell as well as my mother would have liked and sometimes she got attached and had trouble letting them go.

"Just look at their little faces," my mother would say. "Each with its own personality."

She dressed the bears in little caps and matching vests and bow ties and sometimes, when she thought no one was around, she talked to them like they were people.

One day my father called me in New York to say he'd found my mother on the couch, bears all around her like a group of preschoolers waiting on a story.

"She's never been right since that menopause and now she's full-on crazy," he said. He'd caught her complaining to the bears, something about him, the way he gummed a ham sandwich instead of putting his teeth in, the way he chewed with his mouth open and would mow down her rose bushes if he could, mark her words.

"Certified nut ball," he said. "You don't even know because you can't see it, you don't live with it, but I have to."

Now my father is gone but most of the bears are still here, lined up on that same rose-covered couch, their plastic eyes taking it all in – my mother in her obscenely cute shirt, Gina, the bags of seafood, me.

"What the hell is that?" my mother says, pointing at the bags. "Don't tell me you brought fish."

"The best for you, Bert," Gina says. "We've got shrimp, a little lemon sole, some clams."

"You'll stink up my whole house with that," my mother says.

Her hand goes to her hip. She stands between Gina and the rest of the house, blocking. One side of her hair is flattened from a nap. The other side is curled, wired tight as a Brillo pad.

"Crab legs, too," Gina says, and steps around her. "I know you like those. But margarine, no butter, o.k.? Doctor's orders."

"You come here to stink up my house. It's going to smell like the greasy spoon," my mother says. "You bring fish and I'm supposed to be happy?"

"Relax, Bert," Gina says. "We'll take care of everything."

"Relax," my mother says. "While you two stink up my kitchen and make a mess with my pots and pans." She turns around, walks back to her bedroom, and slams the door.

"Sorry. This is what I'm talking about," I tell Gina. "What am I supposed to do?"

Gina holds up the bags of seafood. "Eat," she says, and heads for my mother's kitchen.

The teddy bears glare from the couch. My mother keeps the bears lined up according to color, darkest to lightest. She poses them with their arms around each other, like dancers in a kickline.

Back in her room, my mother slams drawers. She turns up the volume on her black-and-white TV. She cranks up a fan.

Chapter 14

Weekdays I teach my classes, then I go home. I check the Critter Control traps and play "Jeopardy" with my mother. Wednesdays, we eat meatloaf. Mondays, we clip coupons and hit the grocery sales. We visit doctors and pharmacists. We play Scrabble. We sort my mother's pills into little plastic pill dispensers with separate compartments for each day of the week. On weekends, I'm in bed by 11 p.m. I'm up by 9 a.m., my mother singing and snapping blinds. I'm o.k. with this. My mother's o.k. with this. It's manageable, peaceful.

And so when my friend June calls to say she wants to throw Hemingway a party on what would have been his 100th birthday, that she's planning the party for next weekend and expects me to be there, I tell her I'm not up to it.

"What's to be up for? We'll get everyone together to drink and eat and read Hemingway aloud," she says. "It's not like you have anything better to do."

"*The Wizard of Oz* is on TV," I say.

"I'll put you on the list," June says. "Oh, and Dave Newman will be there."

June has been trying to set Dave and me up for years. It never works. There's no way it could work now. It's not just my mother. Even the possibility of love, of a relationship, makes me tired. It's something to delete, a blinking light on an answering machine, a memory.

"I could stick a needle right here and not even feel it," my old boyfriend said, pointing at his scars.

This is what I've become – numb, cauterized, done with all that.

"I can't," I say to June, but she's already hung up.

<>

The party will be at Hemingway's Bar in Oakland. Hemingway would never drink there. This Hemingway's has a menu featuring Buns and Apps. It has frat-boy bartenders who make drinks called Dirty Bong Water and Slippery Nipples. It does not have a jukebox. It has an electronic golf game and big ferns that hang from the ceiling like lynched Muppets.

The last time I was there, a guy tried to pay for his beer with rolls of laundry quarters and a girl asked where she could get souvenir underwear with Hemingway's face on the crotch.

"You know," she told the bartender, "the cute ones, where he's all serious and wearing the turtleneck?"

"It used to be a good place," June says to explain why she still goes there, and she's right. I used to go there in the early 90s when I was in graduate school. Every Tuesday night, in a room off the back, there were poetry and fiction readings. There were no Buns and Apps. There were cheap pitchers of beer. There was a dart board.

I'd show up in a black leather jacket, pretend to smoke, and practice what it meant to be a serious artist with other grad students who were practicing too. We'd say things about deconstruction, postmodernism, the patriarchy's ongoing attempts to homogenize difference. I'd come home from lectures with titles like "The Phallocentric Oligarchy and the Impetus for Empowerment" and weep into my futon.

Then I'd call Gina for advice.

"How am I supposed to learn anything," I'd say, "when I can't even understand the words?"

"Just act like you know," she'd say, "and nobody will know you don't know."

I knew what my father would say. "Phonies," he'd say. "Can't sort shit from shine-ola."

But I wanted to fit, and so I tried on this life like a skin. I made up words. I figured sounding smart might just be a matter of suffixes. Add a centric, an ism or an ization to almost any word and it sounds academic.

"What we have here," I might say, "is the failure of the academicization of the Americancentric lingua francanism to communicate."

This is against everything I believe. It's against everything Hemingway believed. "Faulkner thinks I don't know the 10-dollar words," Hemingway said. "I know the 10-dollar words. But there are smaller, better words and I choose to use them."

Clarity first. Write one true sentence.

"Jackasses," my father would say. "Shit sandwiches."

What did we know? We were all faking our way into lives we hoped would one day be real.

"You're not getting out of this," June says the day of the party.

I've been dreading it, but by the time I get dressed, I'm surprised. I feel relieved to have a night out. It helps that Aunt Thelma has come to stay with my mother.

"I won't be gone long," I say.

"Don't worry about us," Thelma says. "*The Wizard of Oz* is on. It's our favorite. And I brought some other old movies. We'll just curl up on the couch and watch them until one of us snores."

"Don't drink and drive," my mother says. "Don't stay out all night." When I leave, she stands at the door, arms across her chest, the way she used to do when I was 16. She doesn't wave.

At Hemingway's, June has saved a seat for me at a back corner table and I'm grateful. These literary things still make me nervous. I love writers, but as a group, we're insecure, which means we can be cruel, insincere, snobbish, competitive, snarky.

There's a litany of slights that rolls through my head whenever I'm around other writers. "Never heard of it," an Ivy-League alum said when I told her where I went to undergraduate school. "And you call that a poem why?" a professor said in my first writing workshop. "If you're such a feminist," a red-lipsticked fiction writer in elbow-length gloves once said, "why do you look like a Barbie doll?"

Just a few years back, when I was still working for the airlines, I showed up at a writers' conference in Pittsburgh. A guy I'd gone to grad school with who was the literary equivalent of an air drummer, always tapping out the syllabics of poems using a pencil and any available surface, especially his own teeth, came up and said, "Dear god, what are *you* doing here? Are you still *flying?*" He made a little flapping gesture with his hands, right around his fat little cheeks, like his whole face was about to take off. Then he laughed and walked away, one hand slapping iambic on his pleated Dockers.

"I could never be with another writer," I tell June again and again, and she tells me, "You need to be with another writer. You just have to pick the right one."

Now at Hemingway's, all these years later, I still feel open and vulnerable. I put my head down and weave the room and scooch into my seat.

"Hey," a familiar voice next to me says. "What are you going to read?"

It's Dave Newman. Of course June has saved me a seat right next to him.

Dave Newman has been at the bar. He looks the way he always looks. Happy. Pleased with himself, as if he thinks the whole world is a punch line. He's ruddy-cheeked, in a plaid shirt and work boots. Since graduate school, he's been driving a truck. He's gone on writing, but in the cab of a semi he drives back and forth between Iowa and Michigan. The semi, he says, is parked nearby, in a grocery-store parking lot.

"Hemingway," he says, to explain how he ended up here.

He is, by all accounts, a horrible truck driver. I've heard stories – how he's taken the roof off a Pizza Hut, how he's backed his truck over a boulder and had to be lifted off by a crane. He is also, by all accounts including my own, a great writer. Gritty like Celine, one of those French writers I pretended to read in grad school but didn't until I was older. Only Newman is grounded here, in Pittsburgh, our home country. Nearly everything I've read by him is about leaving or coming. And right now, this great writer and terrible driver is home, sitting next to me, with four bottles of beer lined up in front of him.

"The waiter's nice but a little slow," he says, and for the first time I notice his eyes are very blue.

Across the room are writers we've both known for years. One guy is dressed all in white, like Tom Wolfe. Another is in a hat and scarf a la Capote. Another tries to pass herself off as a boxer. When she talks, she makes little punching motions in the air. She's probably read that Hemingway used to do this.

"How do you like it now, gentlemen," Hemingway would say as he punched out all the space around him.

"I hear you're having a tough time," Dave says to me, and I can't help it. I tell him everything. I start with my father's death and go to my mother's heart on the operating table. Finally, I say, "I don't know what I'm doing here," and he says, "Where else would you be?"

<>

When it's my turn, I read the last chapter from *A Farewell to Arms*. It's the chapter where Frederic Henry remembers putting a log in a campfire. The log is full of ants. When the log starts to burn, the ants try to get out. They burn. He pours a cup of water on the log. This steams the ants. No matter what, the ants die. There is nothing to do to save them.

I've read this book for years. It's one of my favorites. Each time, this last chapter means something specific and different and true. This is the first time I've ever read it out loud, here in this room where I've been so many times, in front of people who knew me before I lost my father, before my mother got sick, before I left home and before I came back, before I knew anything about the world and my place in it. It's hard to finish. When I do, my mouth is dry. My hands shake. I look up into all those faces and feel exposed.

And there is Dave Newman in the corner.

He raises his beer. He grins and pounds the table.

He says, "Yes!"

Chapter 15

When I get back from the reading, my mother is awake on the couch. Her displaced teddy bears are lined up against the wall. Aunt Thelma snores, head cocked, mouth open. She looks like a Pez dispenser. They're still watching *The Wizard of Oz*, and the sound is loud enough to feel it.

A scene with the flying monkeys is on. I've always been terrified of these monkeys, their Technicolor blue faces, the way they swoop down and pick the poor scarecrow to bits.

"Well, look who's home," my mother says. "It's about time."

"I thought the movie would be over by now," I say, and look at my watch. It's nearly one a.m.

"It's a tape," my mother says. "We watched it. Then we watched it again."

Thelma's done my mother's hair in crooked pin curls. My mother's housecoat is buttoned wrong. She smells like BenGay and is wearing a tube sock on her left hand. Her arthritis has been acting up. Then again, maybe she's fine and just wants me to think her arthritis is acting up.

"What are you still doing awake?" I say and flick the TV off. I forget about the VCR and let the tape play.

"I couldn't sleep," she says, scowling. "Not with you running around at all hours."

"It's early," I say. "I wasn't gone long."

"Whatever," she says, and crosses her arms like a child.

Now I notice her fingers. The fingers of her sock-free hand are orange. Her lips are orange. There are orange fingerprints along the sleeves of her housecoat and orange spots in her lap. I look under the coffee table and find it. An empty bag of nacho corn curls. Cheesy puffs. Family size. My aunt probably snuck it into the house after I left.

I bend down and pick up the bag. I wave it like a flag. "You know you shouldn't be eating these," I say. I put the bag on the coffee table in front of her. I smooth it out.

"You're not my mother," my mother says, and sticks out her lower, orange-tinted lip.

"It might even be good," the doctor suggests during office visits, "to limit her TV watching. No soap operas, very little news. Keep things as regulated as possible. If you see her getting worked up, just change the channel." He suggests alternatives – handicrafts, baking, bird watching, non-competitive card games. "Some people find Solitaire rather soothing," he says.

But my mother is nearly impossible to regulate. If I spend too much time at work, she tries to rearrange her bedroom furniture. If I'm on the phone, she'll try to drag a 20-pound ham out of the basement freezer and up the stairs. If I get too involved with some freshman composition papers or a book I'm reading, she goes into the kitchen and sets some bacon on fire.

And if I stay out until 1 a.m.?

"What do you people do at those things that make you stay out all hours?" my mother wants to know.

I go into the kitchen and check her nightly pills. They're still cozy in their plastic container. I dump them into my palm and bring them to her, along with a glass of water. I hold the pills out and she plucks them off, one by one, like she's pulling the petals off a daisy. She loves me. She loves me not.

"Who died and made you boss?" she says.

She says, "I don't know who you think you are."

She says, "And on a weeknight. Don't those people have jobs?"

"I don't have to listen to you 24-7," she says.

She says, "Don't they have lives?"

I look around the living room. The furniture is dark wood, free of pictures and knickknacks.

"We should put some pictures up," I say.

"I don't want anything to dust around," my mother says. "You know I hate clutter."

The lamps are heavy and brass. The drapes are pleated and peach colored. They look like coffin liners. The whole room looks like a funeral parlor. My mother in lamplight looks dramatic and staged, all gleam and shadow. Her mouth is thin and pulled tight. She is all spite and sorrow, and she glares at me as if I'm responsible.

"Those people should have lives," she says.

"Of course they have lives, Mom," I say.

Dave, his dented semi out in that parking lot, has a life. In a few hours, he'll be off to Iowa with a truckload of lawnmowers. "Have a good trip," I said. "See you soon."

"I'll try not to hit anything," he said. "I'm not sure when I'll be back."

I wonder if something happened between us back at Hemingway's. "He's perfect," June said, looking pleased with herself. "I told you."

And I think yes, something definitely happened. Then I look at my mother, the empty bag of cheesy puffs, and think no, probably not.

My mother notices the VCR. Inside, the tape is still whirring. She bolts up as if she's been bitten. She realizes she's missing the movie. "Now look what you've done," she says, and flicks the TV back on and turns the volume all the way up. Thelma startle-snores, one long gasp, then goes back into rhythm as my mother plops next to her on the couch.

"That static gives me a headache," my mother says. "Turn it down."

The TV is old, a wooden console with dials and knobs and one crackly speaker. It's the same TV from when I was a child. I would sit between my parents, a bowl of popcorn on my lap. My mother would be on my right with her crochet needles. My father would be on my left with a cup of instant coffee. He liked "The Bionic Man." He liked the evening news.

Right before she'd gotten sick, my mother paid a hundred dollars to a local repair shop to have the TV overhauled. The owner thought she was nuts.

"Lady," he said. "You can't even get a good picture on these things."

But he fixed it.

"It's a solid piece of furniture," my mother said. "You can't find a TV like this anymore."

My mother keeps a lot of things. Her old nursing shoes, my grandmother's broken wristwatch, my father's work clothes. His clothes, still dark and heavy with graphite, hang on a nail downstairs in the basement, in the same place they hung when he was alive.

I turn the TV down.

"Not that low," my mother says. "I don't have dog ears."

She says, "I like this part."

On screen, the Tin Man and the Lion are busy re-stuffing the Scarecrow. The Scarecrow has always been my favorite, maybe because he thinks he's a failure, or because he's wise without realizing it, or because he's kind and complicated – clumsy and graceful, brave and terrified all at once.

My mother prefers Dorothy.

"There's no place like home," my mother says.

Thelma stops snoring, stops breathing, then jolts herself awake. She squints at me, then at the clock on the VCR. "Home already?" she says. "I must have just dozed off. Did you have a good time? Did you meet anybody nice?"

My mother slaps Thelma's leg to shush her, then reaches across Thelma's lap for the remote. She squints at the buttons and pushes fast forward. She's in a hurry to get to her favorite part – the end. Dorothy is about to tell Aunt Em about her adventures. Aunt Em won't believe her. She will think Dorothy has been hallucinating, with that bump on her head and all. And Dorothy, she's always had a big imagination. My mother will play this part over and over again.

I ball up the empty bag of cheesy puffs. I wipe the crumbs off the coffee table and take my mother's empty water glass away.

"Doesn't anyone believe me?" Dorothy is saying. "But anyway, Toto, we're home. And I'm not going to leave here ever, ever again."

"Isn't that a happy ending?" my mother says. "It gets me every time."

Chapter 16

I get takeout from The Super Happy Panda Buffet on Wednesdays between classes. The Super Happy Panda Buffet is a grease pit, but it has a decent Szechuan tofu and vegetables. The shrimp fried rice comes, inexplicably, with raisins. The lunch combo is five dollars.

At the Super Happy takeout window, a giant red-and-white cat raises its good-luck prosperity paw. The cat is a Maneki Neko, my friend Kai told me once. Kai is from Taiwan. Now he runs a car repair shop near my old neighborhood in Queens. There's a huge cat just like this one over the counter in his shop, too.

The cat's actually a Japanese tradition. "Whatever," Kai said. "Everything Japanese was first Chinese. Luck is luck."

The Super Happy Panda Buffet cat is electric. Its arm moves up and down. The paw opens and closes. Hello. Goodbye. Its eyes blink. The coin around its neck sparkles like real gold.

"I like your cat," I say today to the boy who hands me my order, but he's already moved on to the person behind me.

I eat in my car between classes and brush rice and soy sauce off the seats. Today, when I crack open my fortune, it reads, "Life is unpredictable. Enjoy the ride." This sounds like my mother, who speaks in fortune-cookie clichés and mixes her metaphors the way bartenders mix drinks.

"Don't put all your chickens in one basket," she says. "Don't count the eggs before they're hatched."

"Sorry honey. I can't," my mother says when I call from my office to see if she wants to go out for dinner. "I have to pack.

"You have to what?" I say.

I haven't been listening. I've been flipping through student essays I've avoided for weeks. Most of them are about dead grandmothers or dogs. The one in front of me is written in the voice of a dog. The dog is angry. He peed on the living room rug. He has regrets, but mostly he feels justified.

"Why do you beet me, with the newspaper?" the dog wants to know. "Does my tale not wag, in joy? Does my bark not pleas?"

The dog is not a strong speller. He has problems with homonyms and comma splices. He's read too much Shakespeare.

"Thelma and me," my mother says. "We're going to Atlantic City tomorrow. Didn't I tell you?"

She didn't tell me, but lately she's been making a lot of plans.

"You're on your own tomorrow," she'll say. "Thelma and I are hitting the yard sales."

"I have to get to bed early," she'll say. "Pep and I are going for brunch."

My mother's friends all have perky one-syllable names. Dot, Pat, Pep, Flo, Barb, Toots. This seems odd, since their favorite shared pastime is scanning the obits and posting death notices on their refrigerators.

"This is just what happens when you get old," my mother says as she tucks another obit under a magnet. "It's like checking the weather."

Considering the obituaries, I should be happy when my mother's focus turns to yard sales, brunch, get-togethers. I should be happy she's getting on with things.

I'm not.

"You should get more rest," I say.

"Do you think you're o.k. to be driving at dusk?" I say.

"Do not get the fettuccini Alfredo," I say. "Anything but that."

And now this.

Atlantic City is 350 miles away. Six hours by car.

"Do you mean one of those overnight deals?" I say, and picture my mother on the road, her suitcase full of pills.

"No," she says. "Five days."

Aunt Thelma got a last-minute deal on a senior citizen bus trip. The package includes bus fare, a boardwalk motel, a baggie of casino chips, coupons for free hot dogs and shrimp cocktails, one buffet dinner, multiple free drinks, and one Vegas-style show.

Now I picture my mother pumping quarters in the slots. Her arm is automated like the Super Happy Buffet cat. Her heart blinks in a smoke-filled casino. There are bells, sirens, showgirls in ostrich feathers, trays overflowing with whiskey sours and cheesy puffs.

"Don't you think that's a little much?" I say.

"It's too good to pass up," my mother says. She sounds breathy, staccato, and for a minute I suspect she's smoking again, sneaking her old Kool menthols, filling the kitchen with smoke rings, then airing the house before I get home.

"Besides," she says. "Your father and I used to do these trips all the time. You know how much he loved Atlantic City. We used to walk the boardwalk and hold hands. You know your father. He loved to hold hands."

I try not to correct my mother when, out of nostalgia or grief or loneliness, she makes her marriage seem like a 1950s TV show.

"Oh your father," she says, exhaling. "He was so romantic."

My father had tender moments, but he wasn't romantic. He and my mother fought a lot. She told her teddy bear legions all about it. And he was jealous. My mother had always been beautiful, with 1940s movie-star curves, and she attracted attention. In our town alone, both I and my father suspected the tax man, the shoemaker, one pharmacist and several neighbors had, for years, been in love with her. This was the reason for my father's handholding: to make sure my mother could never get too far away. He loved to hold hands, especially in public to show everyone she belonged to him.

It didn't get better as they got older. Once, when my mother was in her early sixties and my father was close to seventy, a trainer from my mother's cardiac rehab center sent a card. My mother had been feeling bad about her progress. The trainer was kind, twenty-something, a college student whose taste in gym wear leaned toward purple spandex. The card had an inspirational message from Helen Steiner Rice. It was covered in bluebirds. When the trainer signed it, he added his phone number.

"What the hell is this?" my father said. "What kind of monkey business is this bastard trying to pull?"

My father waved the card in my mother's face. Then he tore it to pieces. Then he pieced it back together with masking tape. When he could make out the number, my father picked up the phone.

"If you ever so much as look at my wife," my father said. "I'll kick your ass into next Tuesday. Are we clear, sicko?"

Then he slammed the phone down and threw the card in the trash. He must have fished it out later because, after he died, I found it hidden in his underwear drawer.

And these days my mother wants to remember boardwalk strolls, moonlight and romance.

"Overnight would be fine," I say. "You could go down, play some slots, walk the boardwalk a little, think about dad and come home. But five days?"

"I'll be fine," she says. "I'll be with family. You can go check on that apartment of yours."

The last time I'd dropped by the apartment to pick up junk mail, I bumped into Simon.

"Oh you're back," he said. Simon is about a foot shorter than me.

His eyebrows line up with my chest. It's overkill for him to avoid eye contact. He was avoiding eye contact.

"Remember when you said I should watch things?" he said, grinding a toe into the filthy hallway carpeting like he was trying to stub something out. "Well, I borrowed some CDs."

"That's okay," I said. "You can keep them as long as you want."

"I took a bunch of my CDs to the record store," he said. "You know, to sell them. And I sort of sold yours, too."

"I don't think I'm missing anything at the apartment," I tell my mother. "I'll probably just stick around and make sure things are good at the house."

There's a pause, silence. "I'd rather you didn't," she finally says.

A spider scurries out from around the pile of papers. I grab a stapler and whack the spider flat on the dog essay. The spider's a smudge, an ink blot.

"What's that?" I say to my mother.

"I'm going to be gone, so there's no point in you staying here," my mother says, and what she means is: I'm not welcome.

Until my mother got sick, I never had keys to my parents' house. Even as a young child, I always asked before I went into the refrigerator. I kept my voice down, my towels folded and squared off. I hadn't thought about this much before this moment. I was adopted – my parents' adopted only child -- so maybe this is all a side effect of that.

The first lesson of adoption is to be grateful.

"You're very lucky your parents were good enough to take you out of that orphanage," one of my other aunts, not Thelma, liked to say. "You should get down on your knees every day and give thanks. You owe them your life, you know. Your life."

The second lesson of adoption is to know your place.

"A place for everything and everyone in a place," my mother likes to say.

I've been, for all my life, my parents' houseguest, a visitor, a welcome visitor and, at times like this one, a necessary visitor, but always that.

I look at the spider I've smashed on my student's essay. One of its legs is still quivering.

"You have your own things to worry about," my mother is saying. "You need your space."

What she's talking about, I don't know.

Chapter 17

When I take my mother to the bus station the next morning, she's giddy. She wears pink lipstick and a purple velour tracksuit. The tracksuit has sequined roses across the chest and back. She looks like a country music star. The roses glint in the sun. The velour picks up everything. My mother runs a piece of masking tape over her clothes, gathering it up into a sticky ball of dandruff, hair and fuzz.

"It's important to look nice," she says. "Some people don't care how they look. Some people would show up in their underwear if they thought they could get away with it."

I'm in one of my dozen black turtlenecks. My jeans are ripped, wrinkled. I'm not wearing makeup and my hair is frizzed. I look how I feel – tired, disoriented, defeated, a caregiver who's losing her patient to the land of craps and slots, a woman beyond the possibility of love and its long highways and truckloads of lawnmowers, a woman who looks in the mirror and thinks, what's the point? The kind of woman who, within a few years, will get a lot of cats. I'm allergic to cats.

"You should wear more color," my mother says, though she's not really looking at me. She works the tape down each leg now, a sound like tearing. "You look washed out. People will think you're not taking care of yourself. They'll think you're depressed."

She hands me the wad of tape and moves toward the bus. I follow behind with her carry-on, an avocado green train case that as a child I thought glamorous. It looks like treasure, the kind of case movie stars keep their makeup in. It has gathered silk pouches, a secret jewelry compartment, and an oval mirror on the inside of the lid.

My mother packed her medicine, makeup, a clean shirt in case of spills, and several rolls of quarters and nickels so she won't have to wait in line for slot-machine change. It's a trick she learned from my father, who used to carry his slots-money around in a tubesock.

All the change has made the case heavy. I follow my mother on board and store the case in a luggage compartment up front behind the driver.

"Make sure you get help with this," I say.

"No way," my mother says, curling her finger into a hook. "I need that with me. Bring it here. These people steal."

I look around the bus. It's half full, all senior citizens who, despite their tennis shoes, couldn't run fast enough to steal anything. One woman near the front tries to read a pill bottle. A man, her husband maybe, is stretched out in the seat opposite. His post-cataract-surgery sunglasses are black and thick and big enough to blind a horse. The bus driver looks in his rear view mirror and frowns. I mouth sorry. Then I pick the case up and carry it back a few more rows to where Aunt Thelma sits.

Aunt Thelma is wearing a velour tracksuit, too. Hers is black, practical, sequin free. Her lipstick is red. It's bled onto her teeth and into the tiny lines around her mouth. I suspect Aunt Thelma was here before the bus. "To make sure we got a seat," she'd say.

My mother points and I put the case under a seat in front of Thelma, who's already doling out complimentary coupons, looking smug and in charge.

"Have a great trip," I say to everyone. To my mother, I say, quieter, "Take it easy, okay?"

"I'll be fine," she says, pounding the vinyl seat like she could soften it up. "After all, I have angels on my shoulder."

My mother with her drama and clichés. At first I think she's being metaphorical, a walking fortune cookie. I think she's talking about my father, maybe, or even about my grandmother. My grandmother was a good gambler. She could scan dozens of bingo cards in seconds. She played with the intensity of an air traffic controller. My father had terrible luck, but maybe the afterlife has given him an edge. Whatever it is, I think my mother means she's getting help from the other side.

Then she stops pounding the seat, looks up and giggles. She points proudly to her right shoulder. It glints more than the rest of her outfit, and I see the angels are literal. They're piled up, an infestation, like ladybugs.

For weeks, my mother's been collecting these angel stick pins. They are popular at grocery and card-store checkout counters. The angels come with inspirational messages like "Your friendship lifts me up on angels' wings," and "You're the angel of my morning," and "Here's your very own angel to help you through."

All my mother's sad, monosyllabic friends collect these angels, too. They send them to each other as gifts. A basket in my mother's makeup drawer is full of them. There are little metal angels and some ceramic ones with red cheeks and lips. There are angel pins that double as magnets. They hold up the obituaries and bad laminated poems on my mother's refrigerator. There are angels attached to the pull strings on all her lamps. She's stuck angels on her shower curtain and on the lapels of her coats. There is an angel prayer card glued to the car dashboard and angels huddle like barflies on the sun visors.

"Someone's looking out for me," my mother says, glancing out the window now, already moving away from me, free and on the road. "Don't worry."

I look at my mother, the gaggle of angels on her shoulder, and think about Gina, all her little virgins. The things people do to hold back fear.

My father held onto my mother's hand because he was afraid to lose her. She lost him instead. He never thought about that.

Chapter 18

The summer I was six, my father tossed me in the deep end of the pool at the Wilmerding YMCA. Six years later, he took me to see *Jaws*.

"I thought she'd bob up, like an apple," he said about the first incident.

"Christ it's only a movie," he said about the second. "That shark didn't even look real."

Now I doggy-paddle like a pit bull. I breaststroke like a frog in mud. I've read Peter Benchley's novels and every National Geographic story on ocean predators. I do not miss Shark Week. I am a fan of all the Cousteaus. I am knowledgeable about drowning. I am knowledgeable about sharks, which means I'm terrified.

I never had to worry much about a real shark encounter, though, because on all of our annual vacations to Florida, we rarely made it to the beach. My mother hated, still hates, the beach.

"All that sand," she says. "It gets in everything and you can't get it out."

"Seagulls," she says, shuddering, "Filthy birds."

"And those people," she says, "with their asses hanging out. They need their heads examined."

And so we spent most of our vacation time at theme parks and buffets. And we were all okay with that. But then *Jaws* came out, and a few months after I'd seen Quint swallowed whole, when we were peaceably holed up at the Days Inn in Fort

Myers -- my mother in her green bikini with the lace-up top, my father in his plaid swim trunks, me lolling around the shallow end on the back of a raft shaped like an alligator -- my father, who believed fear kept people safe, decided to test things.

"Let's hit the ocean," he said, and he was smirking.

"You know I hate sand," my mother said, her face hidden under a floppy beach hat and white cat's eye glasses. My father held her hand. He bent down and lit his cigarette off her own. My father smoked unfiltered Pall Malls. My mother had her Kools menthols. This, I thought as a child and still think now, said a lot about them.

My father, in his sweetest voice, said, "Just this once. The kid should see the beach."

"I'm o.k. How about ice cream?" I said and held my grinning alligator raft tight around the neck until its eyes bulged. "How about the zoo?"

"Don't be ridiculous," my mother said, and I wasn't sure whether she was talking to my father or me.

My mother leaned back and blew smoke rings. They floated off, a stream of tiny life preservers.

"Come on, princess," my father said. "Be a sport. This will be fun."

<>

It was not fun. At the beach, I dug my toes into the sand and scanned the waves.

"What the hell?" my father said when he saw me far from the water, digging a moat around my beach towel. "You're not even going to dip a toe in?"

I could tell he was happy.

My mother, reconciled to the sand-filled hour we'd have to spend being dive-bombed by seagulls, figured she'd show me. She took off her beach hat. She pulled on her bathing cap – a pink rubber number with wriggling daisies.

She looked like a mental patient in a water ballet.

She looked like a woman with a puffer fish on her head.

"Don't be a chicken," she said. She tucked her arms into wings and did knee bends. She strutted and cawed out into the water.

I was about to tell her not to splash, that sharks love warm and waist-deep water, that Florida was the shark-attack capital of the world. That Florida was where things happened.

And then something happened.

There was a fin. It was large and black and came within a foot of my mother. Then it went back under.

I screamed.

My mother shook her daisy head.

"Chicken," she yelled. "Chicken of the sea!"

The fin came up. The lifeguard adjusted her cleavage. My father fiddled with his transistor radio. The fin splashed down and came up again, followed by a fat man in snorkeling gear. In his right hand, there was a net full of crabs. He flopped from the water like a giant bean bag. His flippers were black and shiny fins.

"We're having seafood tonight," he yelled to his wife, who waved back.

By then I was sobbing.

"I thought you were dead," I told my mother.

"Don't be ridiculous," she said. "We're on vacation."

Chapter 19

I cancel my classes and spend the five days my mother is gone holed up at the apartment. The chair has mostly stopped stinking. Simon returned a few of my CDs that didn't sell. The bathtub is deep and good, bad plumbing aside. I take a bottle of wine and stacks of books in the bathroom with me. I stay in the hot water until my skin shrivels and I nearly pass out.

I have more papers to grade. I should be writing. For years, I wrote poems because I loved to write them. Now I have to write and publish a book to keep a job, and I can't seem to get started even though I have time, space.

I don't want time and space.

"Come out for a drink," June says when she calls from a bar across the street. "It will do you good."

June knows I've been skipping my classes. She knows I haven't been writing. She works at the same university as me and will head up my tenure committee in a few years. She's given me a checklist, things I have to do to keep my job. Write and publish are at the top. Buy lipstick is at the bottom. June believes in balance.

"I am drinking," I say.

"Come out and drink with me," she says. "It's better."

"I'm in the tub," I say.

"Call when you get out," she says.

"I probably should write," I say.

"I'll probably still be here," she says.

"O.k.," I say. I hang up and turn the ringer off. When I get out of the tub, I unplug the answering machine, too, even though there haven't been any messages. Then I think about emergencies and turn the ringer back on, plug the machine in.

I sleep a lot. In between, I think about calling my old boyfriend back in New York, then realize how pathetic it is, the illusion of not being alone.

I had a neighbor years ago, Mrs. Bitner, a crazy lady who lived alone in a big rundown house in Erie. Mrs. Bitner was married once, I think. Her husband died, I don't know when. When I met her, her hobby was cutting pictures from magazines. She autographed the pictures herself and put them in photo albums she liked to show off. "To Edna, Love, Jimmy Carter." "To Edna, With the Beautiful Green Eyes, Love Frank Sinatra." "To Edna, With Admiration, Signed The President."

"See," Mrs. Bitner would say as she flipped through page after page. "Everybody loves me."

I miss my mother, her demands. She's impossible, but at least when she's here I have a purpose. I can bring soup. I can take her to the grocery. I can help sort coupons. I can help with her heart, get her to the doctors and the pharmacy, haggle with the insurance company.

Without her, I'm not sure what I am. A single woman. Not a particularly useful or stylish one. A professor who doesn't teach, a writer who doesn't write. I think about Dave Newman, the poet who drives a truck, and how if I were him I'd never come back. I'd just stay out there. I'd keep moving. It's what I loved about flying, too. If I had my way, if things were different, I'd never hold still in any place long enough to feel a thing.

"It's okay to grieve," June said at my father's funeral. She held me close. She pushed my head against her shoulder. She said, "It's okay. Let it out."

But I couldn't.

There was my mother, holding onto my father in the casket.

There was my mother, weeping until she couldn't breathe.

Someone had to help her up. Someone had to calm her. Someone had to walk her out to the car and away from all that.

Chapter 20

The sweatshirt is off-pink. It has shoulder pads.

"The shoulder pads make it slimming," my mother says. "And it's not pink. It's burnt salmon."

We sit on my mother's bed, two co-eds at a sleepover. My mother is still dressed for the boardwalk – another velour track suit, running shoes, the good necklace she bought on a trip we took to Greece years ago.

The necklace is a pendant, a tiny red-and-gold cloisonné egg from a gift shop in Santorini. The shop specialized in egg necklaces and sea sponges and was perched at the top of a mountain. We climbed dozens of steps to get there, stopping and starting all the way for my mother to catch her breath.

"Wait at the bottom. I'll go," I'd said, but my mother, who didn't have much good jewelry, who'd set her heart on this egg because her friend Dot had smugly come back from Europe with one and my mother was tired of Dot thinking she was better than everyone, had said, "I don't trust your taste. I want to pick it myself."

Now the necklace settles into the tiny indentation in her throat, a nest. My mother looks thin, but happy. She puts the sweatshirt up to my shoulders, measuring. I take it from her and hold it at arm's length.

"Thanks, Mom, it's perfect," I say.

It takes a while to realize where I've seen this shade before. It's the color of the sawdust janitors in elementary schools use when someone pukes in the halls.

I start to fold the sweatshirt back into a plastic bag labeled "Slots A Lot."

"Aren't you going to try it on?" my mother asks. "I got it in a large."

I do not wear pastels. My mother knows this. Black, of course. Brown, fine. The occasional gray. It's been almost 20 years since I've considered anything pink, let alone burnt salmon. I'm a size-medium. I'm sensitive about this. My mother knows that, too. Shoulder pads went out in the 80s. Shoulder pads make ordinary women look like Russian mobsters. I'm not athletic. I do not own sweatshirts, not even a hoodie. I take the shirt back out of the bag, unfold it and slide it over my head. The shirt smells flammable. It's probably the
puffy paint. "Atlantic City is for Lovers" is scrawled across the chest. There is a glittered puffy-paint heart on one sleeve.

"Get it?" my mother says. "You wear your heart on your sleeve!"

She says, "Now isn't that clever!"

She says, "I knew it. Any smaller would have been too tight."

She says, "A little color perks you right up. Every day isn't a funeral, you know."

Along with the sweatshirt, she's brought me a lucky number 7 keychain and a baggie of toiletries she swiped from her hotel. "I asked for extras," she says. "Smell the shampoo. It's cherry. Lucky cherries. Everything's lucky out there."

Maybe it has something to do with the angel pins and divine intervention. Maybe the Greek egg necklace does what the Santorini gift shop owner promised. Maybe it wards off evil and brings good fortune and second chances. Whatever it is, my mother had been lucky out there. For the first time ever, she hit - - $250 in nickels on a Wild Cherry slot machine.

"The machine was spitting it out like popcorn," she says. "All the lights were flashing, a siren was going off. I thought I was going to have a heart attack."

"Not funny," I say, rubbing the puffy paint heart.

"Figure of speech," she says. "You worry too much."

Later, Aunt Thelma comes over and rats her out.

"She didn't feel good," Thelma says. She wears a sweatshirt exactly like mine, same puffy heart on the same sleeve, but in blue. Blue, my mother says, is Thelma's color. It's my mother's color, too. In her closet, there's a spectrum, every shade of sky.

Right now, my mother is in the kitchen, puttering with the tea pot. Thelma and I are in the living room. Thelma's dramatically keeping her voice down. She crouches down to match her voice and I have to stoop to hear her.

I think my mother and her sister imitate old movie stars. Or maybe it's just people of their generation have a more over-the-top way of doing things. "We lived through the Depression," my mother likes to say, as if this explains everything.

"She stayed inside and slept a lot," Thelma says. She looks like a turtle, her chin covertly tucked down and nearly lost inside her sweatshirt. "She was too tired to walk on the beach."

When my mother comes in with cups of tea, Thelma sits up straight and changes the subject. "The crab legs," she says. "They were all you can eat. Really fresh, big piles of them, and so sweet they melted like butter."

"Just like butter," my mother says, and she's looking at me.

Chapter 21

.

"You know I hate the beach," my mother says. "Stop treating me like a child."

"Stop spying on me," she says. "I deserve a little vacation."

"What did you think was going to happen?" she says.

She says, "It wasn't butter. It was margarine."

She says, without a bit of irony, "You're not the boss of me."

And this is when she suggests I stop staying at her house every night.

"Don't be ridiculous," I say. "That's why I'm here. You can't be here alone."

"I most certainly can be," she says. "This is my house." Then, more gently, "You'll be here if I need you. I know that."

I follow her to the living room closet, where she shows me the box. For some time, she's been packing it. The box is full of supplies for my apartment. A parting gift.

"You've been planning this?" I say.

She says, "There was a special on paper towels. Buy one, get one."

When I unpack the box back at my apartment, I will find the paper towels. I will find rolls of toilet paper, a set of tea mugs, a box of sugar wafers, a tin of tea bags, some washcloths and a set of dishrags with ducks on them.

"You want me to go now?" I say to my mother as she motions for me to pick up the box and opens the door.

"It's time we get on with things," she says.

"Not right this second," I say. "We need to see what the doctor says about this, if you're ready."

She says, "That doctor," and sighs.

She says, "No time like the present," and waves me to the door.

The air outside smells sweet, my mother's roses. She's planted them alongside the house. She and my father used to fight over these roses. He hated to mow around them. "Too much trouble," he'd say, and she'd say, "Well, so are you."

Once, on accident I think, my father mowed one over. My mother never let him forget this. "You kill everything good," she said to him. "You kill anything that makes me happy."

My mother leaves the tags on all the rose bushes so she can remember the names. Pink Maiden. Lady's Blush. Sunny Knock Out. To replace the bush he cut down, my father mail-ordered a rose bush named after my mother. The Alberta rose is red and open, like a poppy, with a tiny sun burning at the center. "It doesn't look like much of a rose," my mother said, but she was smiling, happy as always to get her way.

There's nothing else to do, so I carry the box out to my car, past the roses, past the hummingbird feeder my mother keeps full of red sugar water. She comes out to the edge of the porch, but that's as far as she'll go. She lets me kiss her cheek but doesn't kiss back. She makes a dramatic sweep with her arm. "Go on," she says. "I'll call you later."

The egg necklace bobs against her neck, a tiny heart.

Back on Santorini, in that shop on top of the mountain, my mother flirted with the owner. He looked like a fisherman in his little cap. He could have been 60. He could have been 80. They looked into each other's eyes as they haggled over prices. She told him she liked his hat. He complimented her sweater, her good taste.

"Red," he said as she looked over the necklaces, "is the best choice. Though I think you know this."

He took my mother's hand, cupped it between his own, and told her a story I think he told often as part of his sales pitch. The story was one I'd never heard -- about Mary Magdalene, who, after she'd witnessed Jesus' resurrection, went to tell others. No one believed her. They thought she was mad, a mad and wanton woman. And so she did something odd. She started to carry an egg with her wherever she went.

"She'd tell people, 'I know, I know. The idea that someone could rise from the dead is crazy. As crazy as this egg turning red in my hand.'"

The shop owner opened his hands and set my mother's fingers free like a small bird.

"And the egg," he said, "turned red in her hand."

This symbol of resurrection, of faith, a blood spot at my mother's throat.

On the porch, she puts her hands on her hips and anchors down.

She says, "You have your life. I have mine."

"But I don't," I say, and can't tell whether she hears me or not.

Chapter 22

"I think my mother broke up with me," I tell Gina. We're sitting at a card table in my kitchen. We're eating the sugar wafers. They're the cheap good kind, pink on one side, yellow on the other. We drink Earl Grey tea. The tea tastes like perfume and weeds. It leaves an oily slick in my cup.

"You'll get over it," Gina says. "She's tough. She'll probably be fine."

Gina pulls her wafers apart layer by layer and scrapes the filling out with her bottom teeth. "You'll be fine, too," Gina says, and runs a finger over her teeth. "Probably."

Yesterday before I left, after I stuffed the box with the paper towels into the car, I snuck back into the house and programmed my mother's phone so she could push 1 to call me, 2 to call the ambulance, 3 to call Thelma and so on. There was a phone next to her bed, another one in the kitchen. I checked the batteries in her smoke detectors. I checked the gas jets on her stove. I checked her pills, covertly, to make sure the right ones were in the right compartments.

"Come on already," she said. "You're making me nervous."

Useless, a failure in every way, I watched my mother in my rearview mirror until I turned off onto the highway and left her out of sight.

I spent last night not sleeping, rolling through the possibilities of what might happen. I imagined my mother fallen out of bed, her limp hand reaching for the phone inches away. I imagined her dead in the living room, in front of the TV, *The Wizard of Oz* blaring. I imagined she'd wind up like my uncle, the bachelor banker of Braddock, who died alone in his house. Nobody found him for days. "The newspapers were piling up," his neighbor who finally called 911 told my father. "He loved his *Business Times.*"

This morning, Gina came by with gifts – an aloe plant, a fresh can of Lysol in case George's stinky chair acts up. She's here now to help me unpack, alphabetize books, arrange clothes in the closet according to shades and textures of black.

"One of these days, this place might look like someone could live here," she says and pours more tea.

"It's just temporary," I say.

"Everything's temporary," Gina says, "if you think about it."

The light blinks on the answering machine. My New York boyfriend. He's a little drunk, lonely. He's changing careers. He took the test for the police academy. He passed. He wants to celebrate. He keeps calling.

I still have my flight benefits. He knows this. We can go anywhere in the world. There were t-shirts flight attendants used to buy from the company store. The shirts said, "Marry Me. Fly Free." On the machine, his voice says, "What do you say?" He says, "I say Paris. Maybe Madrid." He says, "You have the right to remain silent." He says, "Call me."

Behind Gina, leaning against the wall, there's a piece of art – something Simon made, penance for selling my CDs. It's an old window pane, salvaged from someone's trash. I found it propped against the door, along with a stack of hardware store flyers and a note that said, "Sorry." Simon painted a huge black eye on the glass. The eye has very long lashes and a pupil big as a beach ball.

"Get it?" he said when I saw him in the hall and said thanks. "The eyes are the window to the soul."

"How clever," my mother would say.
She'd put it on a sweatshirt.

Chapter 23

After a few weeks I give in and call New York. I can't explain this. I make plans to spend the weekend with my old boyfriend in Madrid. Madrid is one of my favorite cities. I'm lonely. My mother is determined to be as independent as possible. There's nowhere else I need to be.

"What took you so long?" the boyfriend wants to know, and I say, "I've been busy." My mother, work. I go on a while. He doesn't say anything. I can hear him shuffling paper. I can hear him scratch his cheek.

"I'm the dark, silent type," he'd said with a John Wayne accent when we first met. I thought it was funny. It isn't funny. What he meant is he broods. He doesn't trust anyone. He believes if he lets silence hang, people will eventually fill it up with words and incriminate themselves.

Years later, he'll become a great cop in New York, where this side of his personality will help him get promotion after promotion. "A real cop's cop," his chief will call him.

When we lived together, he would booby-trap things, his dresser, his journal, the box of cash he kept hidden under sweaters in the closet. He'd use dental floss or bits of thread. He'd check to see if anything had been moved, if I'd been snooping.

"I'm a smart man," he'd say and tap his own head like there was a CD in there and it was skipping. This was something my father used to do, too, whenever he felt anyone doubted him. "I know some things," my father would say.

What the boyfriend, Manny, thinks I'm doing in Pittsburgh, I don't know. Or I do know, but refuse to believe it. It's possible he thinks I've made it all up to spite him – my father's death, my mother's illnesses, my need to be here instead of there. Even if he doesn't really believe it's all an intricate hoax, he is the kind of person who might believe such a thing. This is a good reason not to go back.

Still, I'm going back.

I lie to my mother, who hates my boyfriend the way she hated my first husband. "When it comes to men," she said. "You don't have two cents to rub together. Manny is a real jackass."

"You sound like dad," I said, and she said, "Your father knew some things. More than you."

I stop by my mother's house after my last class to tell her I'm spending the weekend at my friend Carol's in New York, the best lie I can think of. I've signed her up for Life Alert, and hand over the beeper necklace I've wrapped up in a velvet jewelry box, like it's something beautiful, a gift.

My mother carefully unwraps it. She lifts the necklace out of the box with two fingers, like it's poisonous. She refuses to put it around her neck.

"It will make you feel safer," I say. "You push the button and an ambulance will come."

"I feel safe enough," she says.

"Do it for me," I say.

"No," she says, and stuffs the beeper into the junk drawer in her kitchen. The drawer's filled to bursting with her collection of rubber bands, twist ties, once-used plastic bags, take-out menus, expired coupons.

"I don't like heavy things around my neck," she says. "I'll look ridiculous. I'll look like an old person."

"You'll never find that in there," I say, but when I reach for the drawer, my mother slaps my hand.

"That's my business," she says.

She says, "I have plans this weekend anyway. Thelma

and I are doing the yard sales. She's in the market for a new kitchen table and chairs."

"Didn't she just get a new kitchen table and chairs?" I say.

"She likes a change," my mother says.

Aunt Thelma likes collecting tables and chairs because she likes people to come and visit. She likes them to sit and stay a while.

"Maybe she's lonely," I say.

My mother says, "What's that to you? She's her own boss. She can do what she wants."

<>

I fly to New York and meet Manny at the Delta counter at JFK. He wears a black turtleneck, black leather jacket, a silver-studded black leather belt. The blue passport in his hand is the only color. He looks like a brushstroke. He looks like he's popped out of a Spanish gangster movie. I'd forgotten how beautiful he is and for a minute I feel my pulse in my throat. Then I see the familiar line of his jaw, the way it flexes when he's angry, impatient, the vein popping like a worm. He must have been waiting a while.

"Sorry," I say, which is how I am with him, always apologizing. I've started to think of him as penance I'm doing.

"I was thinking about leaving without you," he says, and wraps me in a hug. I can feel the muscles in his arms constrict. The leather jacket is warm with its own animal smell, his cologne, the animal smell of him.

The flight to Madrid is wide open. The gate agent puts us in first class. We have champagne. He makes a toast. "It's about time," he says, and I think about Gina, the sugar-cookie icing on her teeth. "Everything's temporary," she said, "if you think about it."

He takes a piece of my hair between his fingers and twirls it, examining the ends for splits. He used to tell me stories about his mother, when she was young, with hair past her shoulders. He said she used a cigarette to burn off her split ends, cauterize them. "She was very beautiful once," he said. "Men look better as we get older. But women." He clicks his tongue against his teeth like a deadbolt.

I imagine I've gone gray overnight, a brittle old useless thing. He lets my hair drop and looks past me, out the window where the clouds beneath us are so thick they seem impenetrable.

How ridiculous to think changing continents could change anything. Still there's comfort in what's familiar, even if what's familiar isn't good. I put my hand on Manny's leg and he puts his hand over mine and keeps it there, like something he's caught.

Chapter 24

In Madrid, we stay at a pensione owned by a widow. She wears a square of black lace on her head. Her hair is dyed black. Her face is a worn change purse. The top of her head barely reaches my shoulders. She doesn't speak English. My Spanish is passable. Manny's Spanish is perfect. He was born in Chile. His mother never learned much English. I think the woman asks if we're married, and Manny assures her.

"She doesn't want sin under her roof," he tells me later. "Ay Dios mio." He makes a sign of the cross and rolls his eyes. He flashes a smile. His teeth are very white, and I think of the dog I had when I was growing up, how she kept her teeth sharp and white by gnawing on bones and rawhide.

"She doesn't like you," Manny is saying about the widow. "She thinks I could do better. She has a daughter. Very beautiful, she says."

The dog would chew a bone down to marrow. She'd growl and snarl, as if she expected the bone to come back to life, as if she'd have to kill it and go on killing it over and over again.

I say, "You should take her daughter to dinner," and Manny says, "Where's your sense of humor, flaka? Skinny little blonde girl. You're losing your ass, you know. You need to eat."

We eat -- overpriced paella in the Plaza Major. The Plaza, the main square in Madrid, was the setting for bullfights and coronations, the Inquisition and many public executions. Now it's mostly restaurants and tapas bars. The paella's too heavy, thick with olive oil. The shrimp are whole, heads on. Their eyes looked stunned. The antennae poke out of the saffron rice like periscopes.

Manny and I hold hands out of habit. We rarely look at each other. Not yet a cop, not even through with his academy training, he already sits with his back to a solid wall and scans the plaza, taking everything and everyone else in.

We take pictures of each other in front of the statue of Felipe III on his horse. The statue is in the middle of the square. People give directions and navigate the Plaza Major via the horse: "At the ass of the horse, turn left" or "It's a right-corner off the ass."

It's chilly, and I'm wearing my old flight attendant coat, a navy trench too big for me. A young couple offers to take our picture together, but Manny says no and waves them off like they've asked for money. Later, in the pictures Manny has taken of me alone, I'll seem lost and tiny in my military-looking coat, my head under the raised hoof of King Felipe's horse's front leg.

We walk the alleyways around the plaza and end up at Meson de Campinon, the mushroom bar, located directly off the ass of the horse. We drink sangria the bartender ladles from a bucket behind the bar and listen to an old man play Frank Sinatra songs on a Casio keyboard. The man may be 90. He's been here forever, back when I used to work for the airlines and came here on layovers, back when I imagined my entire life differently.

This is one of my favorite spots in Madrid, with its two tiny dark and cave-like rooms. Manny goes up and puts money in the organist's tip jar, an old goldfish bowl. The man nods, his eyes barely open. "Para mi novia," Manny says in Spanish, "Play her a love song," and the old man nods again, but doesn't change the song he's playing.

I order a tiny plate of grilled mushrooms and fried sardines. I eat the fish one after another, those crisp whole silver bodies. I can't seem to get full, even after the paella. I crunch the fish bones down to nothing and flash Manny a smile.

Later, back at the pensione, Manny will want to have sex. He'll suggest I let him tie me up with his belt, a test of trust. I will put him off and hide in the bathroom. I will wait until I hear him snoring, all the sangria finally kicking in. Then I'll take a long bath. The water will be barely warm, but I'll keep it running, to spite the widow and her beautiful daughter. I'll use up all the water in this house.

The next night, on the plane ride home, Manny and I will be separated. The flight will be full. The gate agent will apologize, suggest other passengers might switch seats onboard, but neither Manny nor I will bother to ask.

"What's done is done," my mother would say.

Chapter 25

Back at my apartment in Pittsburgh, Gina says, "What were you thinking?" She says, "Seriously, what gives?"

Today she's brought cloves of garlic and a plastic box of straight pins. She sticks each clove with a rainbow-headed pin and places one on every windowsill. She's also brought a bundle of sage. Now she lights the sage and waves it around the apartment like a torch.

"It's important to clean the energy," she says as the sage burns and crackles and sets off the smoke detector. Gina reaches one skinny arm up and silences the alarm, then waves the sage close to my face, cleaning my energy, too, washing off what's left of Manny.

"Good riddance," Gina says about the breakup.

As for the garlic on the windowsills, she says, "It's good to play it safe."

The sage, Gina says, is purifying. The garlic concept, which I think Gina lifted from Voodoo or Santeria or a made-for-TV special, is meant to ward off general negativity, not something more specific.

"Don't be an idiot," Gina says when I mention vampires. "Like this is about that."

"It could be about that," I say, and she says, "Please, haven't you learned anything?"

This started between us back in college, when we took a class called Parapsychology 101. The class fulfilled a science requirement. This made it a big hit with English majors and other dysfunctional types. We had guest speakers: a telekinetic who bent Gina's house key with his mind, then forgot to bend it back; an ESP expert who used lines and squiggles to psychic-test class volunteers; a medium who communicated with one student's dead grandfather until the student left in tears.

This class was odd, especially because we went to a Catholic university where things like crystal balls and Ouija boards were technically off limits. Every year, the priests on the faculty petitioned to have the course cut from the curriculum, but it was popular, a money-maker, even though the professor, Dr. Y, gave impossibly hard tests full of statistics and minutiae meant to prove the academic rigor of his course.

Dr. Y's favorite saying was "Open your minds to possibility." Most of us failed his tests, but Dr. Y graded on a curve and no one I knew ever failed his class.

"Supernatural phenomenon," Gina said when we both got A's in the course.

"It doesn't make any sense," I said.

"Open your mind to possibility," Gina said.

<u><></u>

The sage smoke in the apartment smells like pot. Gina walks by me, her tiny nub of sage ashing on the floor. She stops, spins, then waves the sage in a figure eight between us, the symbol for eternity.

"That should almost do it," she says and bows.

Chapter 26

Today Gina's voice sounds like sparks through the phone. She says, "There's something I need to tell you." At least I think that's what she's saying.

She's on her cell phone. It is, she likes to note, a top-of-the-line cell phone. Gina has an undergraduate degree in writing, like me, but she also has a Masters in computer technology, which is why she can fix a psychic's computer or build databases for huge corporations. All of Gina's technological toys are top of the line. And none of them, not even her microwave and blender, work.

The phone's connection is worse than usual. It sounds like Gina is calling from an elevator filling up with water.

"I can't hear you," I say, and hold the receiver away from my ear to cut the static.

Then the connection is, miraculously, better.

I imagine Gina, her phone antennae wrapped in aluminum foil, her head stuck out her apartment window, the phone cocked sideways, at an awkward angle, four floors up.

"Listen," she's saying. "I did your cards."

"My shards," I say, even though I can hear her just fine. I'm in a mood. I'm between classes and have just wrapped up a magazine-writing seminar where a student told me, "The trouble with you is you expect us to do all this work."

"Your cards," Gina says. "Tarot. It's important. I thought you should know."

I shove half a cheese Danish into my mouth.

"The tower card," Gina says. "It came up. I thought you should know. I thought you might want to take precautions."

I think about the tower card – the images. Flames, fire, people falling. I think about Sally the psychic, and those little ceramic cats prowling her window ledges.

"Take vitamins," Sally advised me.

"Be open to possibility," Dr. Y would say.

I couldn't care less.

Earlier, it had been my mother on the phone. She'd once again forgotten how to write a check. "Do I write out the numbers or the words?" she wanted to know.

She couldn't remember if she'd taken her morning pills. "Don't think I'm losing it," she said. "I am not losing it."

"I'm not helpless, you know," she said.

She said, "You don't need to stay here." She said, "When are you coming home?"

If the tower means confusion, fear, helplessness, if it means wanting to alternately weep and scream, if it means giving up, okay.

"Thanks," I say to Gina. "I will."

In front of me on my desk, the pile of student essays is taller, leaning. A few have fallen off onto the floor, where I slipped on them earlier. My shoe print is clearly visible on the cover page of an essay titled "Mamaw and Me." Next to the phone, is my day's to-do list. It says "Forms. E-mail." It says "Kielbasa. Cranberry juice. Check mom meds." It says "Pay rent. Phone bill."

"It could just mean change," Gina says.

"I'll call you later," I say.

"Be careful driving home," Gina says. "And no heavy machinery."

I hang up. The phone rings. It's Gina again.

"It could just mean change," she says.

I fake the sound of static, bad connection.

Chapter 27

My journalism students are bored. I'm bored, and so I try to come up with a clever assignment to compensate. I'm not sure if Gina would count this as a precaution or not, but I do, something to ward off pointlessness.

The students are supposed to write their own obituaries. Later, I'll think this is morbid, but for now, I think it's quirky and innovative and fun. A lot of my students, after all, will get jobs at newspapers. Their first assignment will probably be the obit desk. The assignment is practical.

"You can invent any life you want," I say. "Or should I say death."

I laugh loud, too long. The students stare.

"Seriously," I say. "What you did for a living, who you married, how you died. Anything. Make it all up. Have fun. Just get the format right. Use Associated Press Style. 250 words or less. Be consistent. And whatever you do, don't misspell your own name."

"I don't get it," one student in a heavy-metal t-shirt says.

"What's not to get?" I say. "Spell your name right. Names are very important in obituaries."

"How am I supposed to know how I'm going to die if I'm not dead yet?" he wants to know.

"Just make it up," I say. "Throw yourself in front of a train. Get eaten by a shark. Go sledding down Everest. Whatever. Just make it up."

"I thought this was journalism," he says. "We're not supposed to make things up."

He rolls his eyes and flops back in his chair. I want to hit him on the forehead. It's a wide and high forehead, a good target. His hair makes him look cross-eyed, birdlike. It makes him look like a pigeon recovering from a stroke.

Seagull, my mother would say, filthy bird.

"Try," I say, and exhale.

"This is fucking stupid," pigeon boy mutters under his breath.

Had I mastered telekinesis back in Dr. Y's class, I could lift pigeon boy with my mind and shake him like a sock. Had I worked on my ESP, I would know what my mother at any moment is feeling and I could step in before things get worse.

Another student, a blonde girl who likes glitter, pokes pigeon boy with a hot-pink pen. It's one of those pens where the ink smells like strawberry. In her obituary, she dies of a broken heart.

"Are we really going to use this in, you know, the real world?" the blonde with her fruity pen says. She often flirts with pigeon boy or tries to impress him.

I want to tell her it doesn't matter, that nothing we do will prepare her for what she calls the real world.

Chapter 28

I was a journalist, just a few years older than my students, working the obit desk when I met Wallace, a man with a name like a comb-over. Wallace and I got married and stayed married for eight weeks.

Wallace was six feet six inches tall. He had a buzz cut, wore shiny mysteriously expensive suits, and had a tattoo of a black-widow spider on his arm. I'm afraid of spiders. I think all buzz-cut men in shiny suits are gangsters. I've rarely lived where the ceilings could accommodate anyone over six feet tall.

Wallace looked ferocious, but he was sweet. He'd been an Army medic. He'd played semi-pro basketball in Germany. He ended up back in North East, Pennsylvania after he hurt his knee during a big game in Hamburg. He slipped on a wet spot that may or may not have been another player's spit.

The spitter got a technical. Wallace got a severance check and a plane ticket home. He worked at his father's gas station and played rugby on the weekends.

"Can't let the knee keep me down," he said when I asked how he could handle rugby, which is much rougher than basketball. Rugby players tend to headbutt things – kneecaps, each other's cars, the pig roasting on a spit after a game. "Anyway," he said. "We're too drunk to feel anything."

Wallace and I had nothing in common, except for one thing.

Years before I met him, before he'd gone to Germany, Wallace had been in love with someone else. It didn't work out. They had a baby, and, when the woman fell in love again and got married, Wallace signed adoption papers.

The little girl grew up a few blocks from Wallace's parents' house. She didn't know about him, but he knew about her. He didn't want to interfere, but sometimes he drove by the house where she lived. Sometimes she'd be playing in the yard. He watched her grow up. When he talked about it, he got quiet and sad, and in those moments, I loved him very much.

As an adopted person, I didn't often think about my birth father, but I hoped he or my birth mother would have cared enough to watch me from a distance. I hoped they would think about me and wonder how I was getting on in the world.

This might have been a good reason to date or be friends, but it wasn't a reason to get married. Still, Wallace, maybe to replace his lost daughter, maybe for reasons that weren't clear, wanted to do just that.

And I was 25 – "a half century" I'd moan to whoever would listen.

So, when Wallace threw a big keg party, when he got down on his good knee and asked me to marry him in front of 25 people who went by nicknames like Balls and Fuzzy, when he slid what may have been his grandmother's and/or his former fiancée's ring on my finger, and when the ring almost fit, I said "Well, okay."

I figured I'd go along with it. Then later, when Wallace and I were alone, in private, I'd gently back out. But I didn't back out. I bought *Bride Magazine*. I bought *Modern Bride*. I started planning. Flowers, invitations, a dress that, if you propped it up just right on the hood of a Volkswagen, would make a great parade float.

I was in love with the idea of a marriage, the way it might look in a bio or an obit, the way it seemed to round out a life. It had little to do with Wallace himself.

This wasn't fair to Wallace, who deserved better, but I did it, and, weeks after a honeymoon in Fort Lauderdale that coincided with a national rugby championship, there were divorce papers to be filled out.

My mother had baked 14 different kinds of cookies for the wedding. She'd overseen the creation of the wedding cake. She'd made sure that, for accuracy, the little plastic bride was scrunched down so that her head hit right around the groom's waist.

"I never liked that jolly green giant," my mother said after the divorce was final.

It was hard to explain what I'd been thinking, or how it made its own kind of sense. After all, no one I knew, my parents included, was happily married. People settled. It's why I stayed with Manny. Settling, I thought -- giving up illusions of bliss and finding a tolerable way through life -- was a sign of adulthood.

I also really liked the dress.

The woman at the dress shop showed me how to use a hair dryer and tissue paper to fluff up the sleeves. The train was cathedral length – overkill for a church-gym reception, but still. In the sunlight, the sequins and pearls around the bodice seemed shot through with rainbows.

"I hope it works out," my mother said, though I wasn't sure if she meant the dress or my marriage.

The day of the wedding, it rained. In pictures, my sleeves are unevenly pouffed. They look dented, like fenders. I ran off mid-reception while Wallace and his rugby cronies wrestled on the dance floor. They threw rented chairs and smashed beer cans off their foreheads. My cathedral train got stuck in the door of my new father-in-law's Cadillac. White silk and taffeta trailed behind as I drove, like toilet paper stuck to a shoe.

I kept running for years. "Fear of death," Freud would say, but he was usually coked up and wrong about many things.

My mother was right about many things.

"What were you thinking?" she said as she wrote a want-ad for the Pennysaver: "For Sale Wedding Dress, Veil. Barely worn."

"I was thinking," I said. "It was about time."

Chapter 29

I leave class, the stack of fake obituaries clutched to my chest like a shield. I try not to make eye contact in the hall. I owe so many students work sometimes they try to corner me to ask about it.

Also, aside from June, I try to avoid many of my colleagues. I'm not supposed to say this. To say this would not be collegial. These are the kinds of words people in academia use. Colleague. Collegial. Collegiality. But I'm a miserable pathetic little person and hardly anyone here likes each other. Scholars who specialize in the 18th century don't have much use for contemporary books and living writers. Most days, I miss being a flight attendant, the physicality of that kind of work, the way even a safety demo, donning a fake oxygen mask and pretending to breathe normally seem more honest than most things here.

Down the hall, directly in front of me, is Corgan Blackfield, the resident Renaissance scholar. He's dressed like a TV professor – tweed elbow-patched blazer, straw hat, a pipe cocked jauntily in one hand. He talks to a student and punctuates the air with his pipe.

Question mark. Question mark.

Corgan speaks with a British accent, even though he's from Illinois and went to college in Ohio. Today he's wearing a pair of binoculars around his neck, and for a minute this throws me. Then I remember: he and his wife, who dresses like a Victorian gardener and loves gigantic tulle bows, are avid bird watchers. "Birders," Corgan says.

The last time I got stuck talking to Corgan, he was very excited about a bird called a gnatcatcher.

"A what?" I said.

"Gnatcatcher," he said, articulating each syllable as if he were shaking a rattle at a baby. "They're actually quite a rare spot."

"My mother keeps a hummingbird feeder on her porch," I said.

"Hummingbirds," he said, his thick black mustache quivering. "Quaint."

I bypass Corgan and pretend not to see him. I pretend to be fascinated by the flyers stuck on the walls. The flyers advertise dances and book sales, beauty pageants and bingo night. There are so many flyers, printed on bright paper and loaded down with glitter, but my students always ask me why nothing is ever going on.

"This place sucks," pigeon boy said on his way out of class.

"I don't know," I said, meaning anything.

I wind my way through the hall, then stop underneath an Army ROTC recruitment poster, the words "Be All You Can Be." I see something familiar. A blue jacket. The jacket seems exceptionally bright, Technicolor, the color of birds in Disney movies.

"A blue gray gnatcatcher, to be precise," Corgan had said.

Above the blue collar, there is a ruddy face and bluer eyes.

It's Dave Newman, from that night at Hemingway's.

"I told you," June had said. "He's perfect."

I'd given up seeing him again, assumed he'd be lost forever in some cornfields in Iowa, delivering lawn mowers and tractors to farm supply stores everywhere. I can't believe he's here, now. I look, look again, and it still doesn't make sense.

"Dave?" I say. "Dave Newman?"

He looks like what he is, rugged, beautiful, someone who knows a life on the road. Under the blue jacket, there's a plaid shirt. He's wearing work boots. His jeans are slack, a little grease-stained. His face looks fresh-scrubbed, and I think for a minute he might be drunk, he looks that happy.

I know a lot about traveling for a living, but I can't imagine what it's like to live half your life in a truck. I know he usually sleeps in the cab, in a space the size of a closet, next to a milk crate he keeps filled with books and notebooks he loads with poems.

When I asked him back at Hemingway's what kinds of hotel rooms his trucking company used for layovers, he'd laughed.

"Motel Six, maybe once a month. About thirty bucks' worth," he'd said. "If we don't get the room, we get to keep the money. I usually keep the money."

When I was flying, a passenger once asked my friend Jaime if we slept on the plane. We thought it was a funny question, and Jaime, a sharp-witted hand model who felt he belonged on a different kind of runway, went at it.

"Absolutely," Jaime said, and he popped open an overhead bin and gestured at it with his catalogue-quality hands. "We sleep in the overheads. Our own little pods." Jaime leaned in and whispered, "We shower in the cockpit. But we have to be careful. The pilots are sneaky. They like to watch." Then he slammed the bin shut and the poor passenger, stunned, silent, toddled off down the aisle, his roller bag dragging behind like a broken Slinky.

"Please," Jaime said. "As if."

It's easy to romanticize my old job, but I haven't forgotten the passenger who told me he'd like to shove the snack basket up my ass. I haven't forgotten the way people handed off leaky airsickness bags and balled-up diapers like they were gifts. I haven't forgotten the proper manicures and dollopy up-do's of supervisors whose viciousness was slicked over with Southern charm.

But our layover hotels were all four and five stars.

For me, being on the road meant a hotel in Athens that had heated floors in the bathrooms. It meant a hotel in Hartford, Connecticut that had steam saunas in each suite. It meant a hotel in Madrid that offered monogrammed slippers and robes and free breakfast from room service.

"You're fucking kidding me?" Dave said when I told him this. He looked disgusted or maybe amused. I didn't know which.

I like nice hotels. I like fancy cheese and the champagne I used to swipe from First Class. I liked telling Dave, "There's nothing like having a Greek salad in Greece," and it was true, though I meant it as funny, ironic. I thought I sounded charming, maybe. Maybe I was showing off a little.

"Miss world traveler," my mother would say. "You can put a pig in a poke but it still stinks."

But I can't afford most of the things I like. Neither could Jaime the hand model, but back then they came with our jobs. Dave's life, his job, is truck stops and strip bars and bargain movie matinees. He eats a lot of fast food. He snacks on moon pies and cake rolls. He pumps up on speed and Mountain Dew. To save time when he drives, he pisses in empty soda bottles. He's written a great long poem about this, and about a favorite diner in Florida, I read the poems in a magazine. In the poem, the waitresses are topless, call everyone honey, and the cook makes the best country-fried steak with white gravy.

"He's perfect for you," June said. "He writes like Bukowski."

Maybe he is perfect, but who knows. For everything we have in common – writing, love of books, music, drinking, Pittsburgh – there are differences between us that are huge and spiraling. Dave has his own set of problems, a recent drunk-driving arrest to deal with.

I suspect he not only writes like Bukowski. He lives like him, too.

So why am I this happy to see him?

Why do I feel someone's opened a window and let the air in?

"It might be about change," Gina had said, and now here it is.

Minutes ago, in class with pigeon boy rolling his blank doll eyes, I felt hopeless, and now I don't.

I drop my office keys, lose a few stray obituaries, and rush to hug Dave Newman, who is right now standing in for everything that's good. I nearly knock him backwards.

Then I catch myself and say, "Are you here to see June? You're probably here to see June. She's still in class. I let mine out early."

He picks up my keys and papers and hands them over. His smile is easy, casual. I'm embarrassed to have made so much of things.

"I'm here to see you," he says.

"Why," I tell my journalism students, "is the most important question you can ask. Why is the real heart of the story. Anyone can do 'who, what, when, where,' but why – why is the human question. A good journalist isn't afraid to become like a child. Ask why. Wonder. Be curious. Be open."

All around us, students change classes, rush out to smoke. I'm blocking traffic, getting whacked with a trailing backpack here and there, but it doesn't occur to me to move. Corgan sidles around us and out the door, binoculars bouncing. "Ta-ta," he says, and salutes as he goes by.

"You should have been here sooner," I say to Dave.

He smells like beer and grape bubblegum. He smells like wind and oil and asphalt. There's a book tucked into his waistband, nestled into the small of his back like a gun. Dave, I know, likes Parra, Neruda. He likes Hikmet and James Wright. I want to know what the book is. I'd like to read more of Dave's new poems, what he's been writing in his truck. I'd like to hear his stories about lawnmowers and strippers and how long they keep the lights on at Motel Six. I'd like to tell him about pigeon boy, about Corgan the birder, about essays written in the voices of Shakespearean dogs.

I didn't know until now how lonely I've been.

"I came straight here," Dave says.

"Where were you?" I say.

"Everywhere," Dave says. "Iowa."

"Well, you're too late," I say.

"For what?" he says.

"I killed myself off last class," I say, really hugging him now. He hugs back.

In my ear, he says, "Killed yourself how?"

Chapter 30

On our way to lunch then a poetry reading, Dave drives. His car is clean, down to the floor mats. There's a trucking map on the back seat and a pack of grape bubble gum on the dash. There's change in the change tray, but it's sorted, all quarters. Not a penny in sight.

My car is a wreck – old coffee cups, mangled student papers, books and cds, wadded-up tissues. There's change, but it's everywhere – in the seats, under the pedals, in the glove compartment.

I'm embarrassed to be in a space so neatly organized. I have to fight the urge to take off my shoes.

"You're very neat," I say, and run my hand over the dashboard in front of me. It's slick, lemon polished.

Dave says, "I appreciate that."

At the poetry reading, we listen to Tony Hoagland. Tony Hoagland writes tough-guy poems, but in person he's tiny. I pictured him in a tank top and jeans. He wears a polo shirt and Dockers. It's hard to connect the person who's speaking with the guy in the poems. The guy in the poems sounds like heavy machinery. The tiny, fragile-looking poet on stage looks like he'd splinter if he sneezed.

Poetry, my first literary love, is like church for me. I don't go to church. I go to poetry readings looking for a spiritual experience. There's no other way to describe it. I want poems to lift me up out of my body in the ways I imagine very religious people feel lifted out of their bodies when they're called to speak in tongues or shout out loud or dip their hands into a box of snakes.

There are many poets who do this for me. On the page, Tony Hoagland is one, but so far in person he is not. I do not feel moved. I don't feel called to weep or shout. Mostly, I'm bored, heartsick about it and trying not to let on. Tony Hoagland really is a wonderful poet, and he might just be having an off night. He goes on reading poem after poem about capitalism and the bourgeoisie, about dogs and white people, about feminism and hedonism and the perfume of fermenting joy. Hoagland's point is he hates isms, I think. He uses them a lot.

In the row behind us there's my poet friend Michael and a guy in a scarf, Michael's new publisher.

Dave and I clap when everyone claps, we're quiet when everyone's quiet. We're two eggs in a carton, two proper attentive heads.

We're careful around each other, the way people are with strangers at first. We sit up straight, we don't sneak off to the bathroom. We're good audience members right up until Dave leans over and whispers, "This about sucks," and, relieved, I grab his hand and say, "We should get out of here," but we're sitting in the middle of a row. We'd have to climb over people to get out. We'd have to block Michael's and his new publisher's view. So we sit back and hold still.

Soon Tony Hoagland is reading: "No matter how you feel you have to act / like you are very popular with yourself / very relaxed and purposeful / very unconfused / and not / like you are walking through the sunshine / singing / in chains."

He's back, and the voice matches up now. The poem and the poet are barreling head on. The reading gets better. Dave and I let our hands and knees touch, our bodies loosen. We lean into each other, and now our shoulders touch too, so we look less like two separate people and more like one solid thing, a paperweight, a snow globe, a breathing cluster, two people in love with words.

<>

After the reading, we go out for drinks with Michael and his publisher, who has a handkerchief in the pocket of his blazer. The handkerchief is silk. It's red. It matches his scarf.

We go to a place in Shadyside where all the tables are wrapped with brown paper and the centerpiece is a cup of crayons. The place isn't kid friendly. There are buffalo burgers on the menu. There's calamari. The crayons are for the grown-ups. At the table next to us, a man and a woman in their 50s play Hangman. They look married, matching rings, mirrored expressions, the same sad lines around their mouths. They seem serious about the game.

"So," Michael's publisher, scarf-man, says to me. "You're in the academy?"

He has large black rimmed glasses, very Elvis Costello. He has the habit of taking them off and wiping them with the edge of his scarf. He wipes each lens over and over, making tiny circles with his scarf between his thumb and forefinger. He wipes, puts the glasses on, takes them off seconds later and wipes again. I think it's a tic, but he doesn't seem nervous or bothered at all.

"I teach," I say. "Writing courses, mostly."

Scarf-man owns his own publishing house. That's what he calls it. He has chosen Michael's work for his first venture. That's what he calls it, a venture. Scarf-man is, I think, independently wealthy, which might explain his lack of self consciousness, which might mean he doesn't have a day job. His publishing house is called Elemenope.

Michael explains, "Like LMNOP, like the alphabet."

Michael is wonderful. His poems, tiny crystallized

moments, glisten on the page. I'm happy he'll have this book out. I'm happy his poems have found a home.

"So what did you think of the reading?" scarf-man asks and I say, "I like Hoagland's work. I thought the reading was good. I liked the last poems best."

"I make a point of not listening to the opinions of anyone in the academy," scarf-man says, glasses off, wiping. "It's so incestuous, the academy, don't you think? I'm interested more in the common man."

"I was a flight attendant for years. Before that, I waited tables," I say. I'm shredding my napkin now, something I do when I'm angry and nervous. Michael's immersed himself in the menu, trying to change the subject.

"How are the mussels?" he says. "Has anyone had the mussels?"

"But you're in the academy *now*," scarf-man says. "This renders you impotent. You no longer have any gauge on the real world, on, say, the everyday zeitgeist of human experience. But you," he says to Dave. "I'm interested. What did you think?"

Dave doesn't answer. He's tossed back three beers. He's nudged me with his knee under the table. Now he's working a crayon. It's blue.

He's drawing a cock on the brown paper tablecloth, covertly, alongside his plate, just out of scarf-man's line of sight. The cock has very hairy balls. It has glasses. It's wearing a scarf. Next to all this is an arrow. It's pointing straight at scarf-man, who's saying, "I am most interested in an altruistic shift of the dominant paradigm."

Dave asks the waiter for our check. He says, "We really have to get going."

If this isn't a reason to fall in love with someone, tell me what is.

Chapter 31

A month passes and we're together in the apartment. Dave is next to me in bed. We eat toast and watch *Annie Hall* on an old TV and VCR he brought with him, along with the bed, when he moved in. The part about relationships being like sharks is on. It's one of my favorite moments.

"A relationship has to move forward or it dies," Woody's Alvy Singer is saying to Diane Keaton's Annie. I go on finishing the lines. I've been doing this through the whole movie, which is probably annoying but I can't help it.

"Do you want me to just turn the volume down?" Dave says, and I give him a shove with my foot.

On the floor, there's a stack of movies we've been watching and re-watching, Dave's copies of *Rushmore*, *Bottle Rocket*, and *Dead Man*, my Woody Allen collection, and good old movies like *African Queen* and *Casablanca*. It's a big stack.

The bedroom windows are open and the sounds of the city come up from the street. Everything sounds hurried, all car horns and exhaust. Movies give us what we think is a legitimate excuse to stay in bed. We know we should be up. It's mid-afternoon. I need to go to see my mother, who knows nothing about this, and check in. I need to get to the grocery and buy something other than bread. But neither Dave nor I want to move.

There's something about new love that goes against what Woody Allen says, at least literally. There's the push to do anything but move forward. There's the push to hold still, stay in the moment, because the moment feels that good.

For now, I like Dave's chest. I'd like to tuck my face under his arm and breathe him in. He smells like sweat and buttered toast and strawberry deodorant. I'd like to never move again.

On the screen, Annie is lovely in her baggy menswear and hats. Alvy's a mess, with his bald patches and a syncopated voice that whines and stalls like a roller coaster being pulled uphill. *Annie Hall* is my favorite movie. I love it the way my mother loves *The Wizard of Oz*.

"Love fades," an old woman on the street tells Alvy, but I look at Dave and I think maybe not. Above us, on the craggy ceiling, there's a water stain. It looks like a fat man in a bowler hat. It looks like Hitchcock has made a cameo right here, in this bedroom, where the floors are so slanted the walls seem to lean into each other, where the only furniture is the bed and this TV and a wooden tray table we use to set plates of toast on.

If we can be this happy here, who knows?

"Well la-di-da," Annie would say.

"This is perfect," I say and blow a breath through Dave's chest hair. It's thick and dark except for one squared off patch near the center. I trace the patch with one finger, trying to memorize the shape, the spacing.

"It is," Dave says, and tangles a hand in my hair. I wrap one leg high around his waist and squeeze. His other hand grabs hold of my foot and his thumb lands on the thick scar that runs up the back of my ankle like a zipper.

I have scars like this on the backs of both ankles, all the way to mid-calf, left-overs from the many surgeries I had growing up. The surgeries started after my parents adopted me. The surgeries were expensive. They fixed my badly clubbed feet, my crooked legs.

I wasn't supposed to be able to walk, then I did.

I don't know how my parents could afford all those surgeries. I don't know everything they had to do without. I know my mother always wanted a new kitchen floor. It was something she and my father argued about. Her kitchen is small, not a lot of floor to cover. It wouldn't cost much, but there never seemed to be money for it. The floor's still there, same yellowed linoleum, and my mother's still angry about it, though no one's telling her now she can't have a new one.

"You wouldn't walk if it weren't for us," my father would say as a rationale for why I should always do what I was told.

"You cost as much as two kids," my mother would say to explain why I was and always would be an only child.

"You should be grateful to your parents," the nuns at school would say.

But it's a hard thing to be reminded of constantly. It's a hard thing to know that life is an owed thing, a debt from the start. I spent years trying not to owe anyone anything, trying not to be vulnerable.

"You know who you have?" my friend Meg in New York likes to say, then she answers, "Yourself."

Meg's mother died when Meg was just a little girl, and Meg never got over this. Now she thinks it saves people to know the truth about things.

"Knowing you're alone lowers your expectations when it comes to other people," she says.

I'm thinking of all this now as a way to explain why, until this moment with this man in this wreck of a room, I've always been, in some mixed-up back-roads stumbling way, protective of my own heart.

"I don't usually have sex or get involved with anyone I really care about," I told Dave the first night we were together.

"That's the stupidest thing I've ever heard," he said, but he was smiling.

I roll words around like dice. Exception. Exceptional. Except.

Dave runs his thumb up and down the scar. He's the only person who's ever touched it without me pulling back. The skin is thin there, sensitive, pale pink, almost translucent. Sometimes I dream I bump my ankles against something sharp and they crack open to the bone.

Chapter 32

Later, we're having sex and Dave wants me to talk. "Tell me what you like," he says. He says, "Tell me what feels good."

But I can't talk. I can't find the words but I want to find the words, something I've never wanted before.

Dave pulls my hair. I'm on my hands and knees. He says over and over, "Tell me," but words take trust. It will be weeks before I'll be able to tell him I'm about to come.

What I know: we're in love, but we're strangers. My mother doesn't know Dave's moved in. His parents don't know about me. This isn't the beginning of a movie romance. Even though it feels perfect, even though I say it's perfect, it's not.

This is what I think about, the tension between what I feel and what I know.

Before the day he showed up on campus, Dave had been living with his parents in Michigan, in their unfinished basement because he couldn't drive. He couldn't drive because he'd lost his license after getting a DUI. The DUI, the inability to drive, cost him his job as a truck driver. This was not promising. Living in the basement was not promising. The floors were concrete. He'd been sleeping on a futon next to the furnace.

"Don't they have a spare bedroom?" I'd asked.

"They're not exactly happy about me being there," he said.

After the trucking job fell apart, he took two other jobs – one for an overnight shipping company where he carried a stopwatch and clipboard, the other substitute teaching in Detroit. He'd been offered a third job as manager of a 24-hour mini-mart.

"In Detroit?" I said.

"I'd get all the free Slurpees I can drink," he said, joking. "I'd have to bring my own cup, though."

"Move in with me," I said, just like that.

Dave said, "Really?" and I said, "I'm sure," though I've never been sure of anything and as soon as the words were out, the fear seeped in.

Dave cashed savings bonds his grandfather gave him when he was born. He picked up his last paychecks. He told his parents he was moving to Pittsburgh for a new job. I didn't know if his license was still suspended or not. He drove and I didn't ask. He moved his dandruff shampoo into the shower, his strawberry deodorant into the medicine cabinet. He cleaned out my car, all the strewn papers and crushed coffee cups, and alphabetized all our books. We merged our books on shelves we bought at IKEA, which seemed like commitment. Only couples who are serious shop at IKEA, all those little pencils and checklists. Only couples who are in love can put the furniture together without killing each other.

"I could never be with another writer," I'd told June, and she'd said, "You should only be with another writer. You just have to make sure it's the right one."

Dave and I have so many books. Many of them are doubles, sometimes triples. I think this is a good sign. On the shelf, there are three *Sun Also Rises,* two of James Wright's *The Branch Will Not Break.*

So why do I feel so uneasy?

"If the universe is expanding," nine-year-old Alvy Singer tells his therapist in "Annie Hall," "someday it will break apart and that would be the end of everything."

"What is that your business?" Alvy's mother wants to know.

Chapter 33

My mother's voice cracks on the answering machine. "Pick up. I know you're there."

She sounds like a manager on a loudspeaker at the grocery. Clean Up, Aisle 17.

I pull a pillow over my head and punch where my face would have been.

"You should get that," Dave says. By now it's late afternoon.

"You get it," I say from under the pillow. "Tell her wrong number."

"Don't be a pussy," he says, peeking under the pillow. I yank it back down.

"It will just get worse," he says. There's a stack of newspapers piled up on Dave's belly and more on the bed. He's looking through want ads, trying to find a job. "You're going to have to tell her sooner or later."

I punch the pillow again, then get up, scattering newsprint, and head for the phone.

"Where have you been? I tried calling all morning," my mother says. Her voice is half whine, half snarl. I think about the sound the raccoons make when they're ravaging her garbage. I think about Critter Control.

"I was worried sick," my mother's saying. "I have soup. I thought you were coming at lunchtime. You said you were coming at lunchtime. I could drop dead worrying and waiting for you these days."

"Tell her we'll be over tomorrow," Dave yells from the bedroom. He thinks this is funny. I pick up the loaf of bread from the counter and launch it into the bedroom.

"What was that?" my mother says. "Is someone there? Is something going on?"

I'm 15 again, terrified and guilty and needing to explain what my mother found in my diary, tucked under my bed, in my closet, in the next room of this apartment where I've gone, in her words – her words -- to get on with things.

"I met someone," I say. So there.

"And he's in your apartment?" she says.

"He's great. You'll love him," I say.

"We had plans," she says. "Tell this him of yours. Tell him that."

"We didn't," I say. "Not really."

"What's his name, this person?" my mother says.

"Dave Newman," I say.

"Is he normal-sized?" my mother says. "Your last husband was not normal-sized."

"Don't start," I say.

"Who's starting?" she says. "He doesn't play basketball, does he?"

From the bedroom, the loaf of bread flies back. It thuds at my feet.

By the time I hang up, I've made the plans my mother and I didn't have before. It's been confusing with her lately. She wants me around when she wants me around. She wants me there, and then she doesn't. It's more than a whim, but I'm not sure what to call it.

"You're not the center of everything," she says, about me, and I say, "You're kidding, right?"

The plan is I'll head over to her house in an hour to take her shopping. Groceries, the pharmacy.

"Giant Eagle has a sale on cauliflower," she says. "Buy one get one. I'll be dressed. I'll be waiting. Don't putz. And tell your what's-his-name, Normal Sized, to come for dinner tomorrow. I want to see this one."

I pick up the bread and put it on the counter. I unplug the toaster and tuck it away. "I'll cook," I say, and my mother says, "You will not. You're not making a mess of my kitchen again. I'm not an invalid. He's not a picky eater is he?"

Dave doesn't eat vegetables. Vegetables for spices, like garlic and onions, have to be pureed down to a paste. He eats meat, an occasional ear of corn. He doesn't eat fruit. His mother used to bribe him when he was a kid, one dollar for every strawberry. He'd swallow them whole, pocket the cash, then puke them back up when she wasn't looking.

"Of course not," I tell my mother.

"I hate picky eaters," she says.

"You're going to love him," I say, and my mother hangs up.

"Well," Dave says, up now, naked, red-cheeked, scratching. He takes the toaster back down and re- loads it. He looks pleased with himself. "So how'd it go?"

<>

I spend the rest of the day with my mother. We hit Giant Eagle, where she picks a fight with the man at the deli counter over whether or not the hot sausage should be orange.

"You people put all kinds of dyes in it to make it look like that," my mother says. "Probably red dye. You're probably trying to give people cancer."

The deli man looks tired. His little paper hat is crooked. There's a smear of what looks like old potato salad and meat grease on his apron. His nametag says Ronald. It says "Our Best is the Freshest Yet."

"Lady, it's spices that make it that color. That's what makes it hot," Ronald says. His hands are huge in their crinkly plastic gloves. They look like they could choke someone, have choked someone.

"Don't give me that," my mother says. "I know sausage. I'm Italian."

She's half Italian.

My grandmother was Slovak. I know a lot of swear words in Slovene. I know how to make a nice stuffed cabbage and once spent a week as a Junior Tamburitzin. I liked the costumes, all those ribbons and flowing skirts, but never could get the hang of having to dance and play a tiny guitar all at once. "It's not in her blood," my grandmother, who never fully thought of me as one of the family, said.

But my grandfather, who died just before I was adopted, was said to be full Italian, though he was orphaned, like me, and spent most of his life in a real orphanage. He might not have considered himself much of anything, ethnicity-wise. He died on his birthday, dropped dead without warning on the sidewalk two blocks from his house, a bad heart, like my mother's. He'd gone to the grocery to get ice cream. His kids loved ice cream.

"Daddy just didn't come home," Aunt Thelma says when she tells the story, and she sounds just like the little girl she was when it happened. Maybe their lost father is why Aunt Thelma and my mother never miss the Pittsburgh Italian Festival. They love Mario Lanza. They have Italian porch flags and matching Kiss Me I'm Italian sweatshirts.

"I know sausage," my mother is saying to Ronald the deli man. "Don't give me your bull."

"Lady, do you want it or not?" Ronald says, and my mother says, "Fine. One pound. Not an ounce more. I know how you people do. And double bag it."

"Sorry. She feels like everyone's trying to get one over on her," I say to Ronald, and he says, "Whatever."

Later, my mother's still stewing in the produce aisle where she's riffling through cauliflower, all those decapitated heads.

"They always do that," she says.

"Do what?" I say.

"Treat old people like idiots. Like we don't know anything," she says. She grabs a cauliflower head and shoves it into the plastic bag I'm holding open for her. She spins the cauliflower head so the bag twists shut and I tie it up.

Chapter 34

When I get back to the apartment, it's late, nearly midnight. Dave's not there. He's gone to meet our friend Bob at a bar called The Shaker. Bob is a poet and a journalist. He works part-time as the Shaker's bartender, which means the drinks are free. The Shaker is attached to a bowling alley in Irwin. Its sign is rusting, faded, and despite the name, the bar's not big on martinis. It's a shot-and-beer place, with Iron City and Stoney's on tap. There's never a crowd, but it has a few regulars, old mill workers who tell good stories, which Bob says, along with the free drinks, makes it a good job.

By the time Dave and Bob get in, it's 3 a.m. I'm sleeping. The bedroom is next to the kitchen. The bed is against the wall that divides the two rooms. The wall is thin, so when one of them, Dave or Bob, bang on it to make a point, the bed shakes. They turn on the stereo. They slam things. I smell cigarette smoke. I start sneezing. They're talking loud over the music. They're reciting poems, back and forth to each other. James Wright and Ed Ochester, I think.

I love Ed Ochester and James Wright but it's 3 a.m. and tomorrow, there's my mother, dinner. "What the fuck?" I say, but no one can hear me.

When I stumble out to tell them to knock it off, Bob is in the refrigerator. He's sitting on the floor with the door open, leaning against the shelves. There's a half-gallon of milk in his left hand and a Tupperware container of cookies in his lap.

"Hey," he says, and toasts me with the milk. "Nice jammies."

My pajamas are blue flannel, covered with clouds, stained with coffee, three sizes too large. I pull my arms across my chest, ashamed, even though I know Bob's drunk, Dave's drunk, and neither of them care or will remember how I look right now.

I walk over to where Dave's sitting on the counter, his legs dangling like a kid on a swing. He's happy drunk. He smells like smoke and stale beer and something else. Doritos, I think, ranch flavored.

He says, "How was your mom?"

I come closer. There's something wrong with his face. His expression looks stunned. It's hard to tell what's different at first, then it isn't.

"What happened to your eyelashes?" I say, because they're gone, along with half of one eyebrow.

He shrugs, smiles. "Flaming shots," he says. "I got too close."

"People under the influence," Bob says in his sagest voice, "should not play with incendiary things." He sounds like a Mark Twain impersonator. He slugs back more milk and it drips down his shirt, a snap-front Western number, plaid, flap chest pockets, at least one size too small.

Chapter 35

The next day looks like disaster.

Dave is hung over. His eyelashes are, of course, still missing. His skin looks grey and his eyelids are red and swollen. His eyes are glassy, bloodshot. He looks like something from the reptile cave at the zoo.

I say, "Maybe I can get us out of this."

He says, "Are you kidding?" He says, "Let's do this."

And I think, what is it we're doing exactly?

There are people who like to drink, and then there's the kind of person who drinks and burns his eyelashes off in an old man bar in Irwin, Pennsylvania. I think Dave might have real problems, things I haven't considered, but I push the thought back down. Mostly, we're happy in bed with our toast and movies. We laugh and talk and this, this eye-hair thing, this 3 a.m. drunk thing, isn't how it is between us at all.

I can convince myself of many things and sometimes this is a good thing and sometimes not.

Dave's in a good mood, despite his looks. He seems actually happy to meet my mother, even after all he's heard from me.

"Don't expect her to be nice," I'd said.

"She's kind of rabid," I'd said.

I'd said, "Maybe we should wait."

Dave shaves and gets dressed in a nice shirt and khakis. "I fucking love you," he says and kisses me hard once on the forehead, once on the lips, and I can't help but kiss him back.

"I apologize in advance for anything that's about to happen," I say.

Dave says, "Sorry about last night."

When we pull up at my mother's house, Dave flips the visor down and double-checks his face. He rubs his lashless eyes, hard, like he's willing the lashes to grow back. Then he turns to me and says, "What do you think? Do I look o.k.? How noticeable are the eyes?"

"Very," I say.

My mother doesn't seem to notice any of it. She's dressed in her good track suit, the purple velour one with the roses, the one she saves for special things like her senior citizen bus trips. She's smiling. She's done her hair in pin curls and the grey swirls make her look almost soft, cloud-like.

When she waves her arm to invite Dave in she says, "It's so nice to meet you." She says, "Welcome to my home." She says, "My daughter's told me nothing about you."

She's set the table Italian-bistro style, a red-and-white checked tablecloth, her good flowered pasta bowls, an empty bottle of Riunite used as a vase for plastic roses.

"It's good for my heart," she says before I ask about the wine. To Dave she says, "My daughter likes to badger."

It's a test. Already she wants him to take sides.

After dinner, after I've eaten the cauliflower off Dave's plate when my mother wasn't looking, after he complimented her on her meatballs and my mother blushed and patted his hand and said, "It's hard to get a good meatball these days," I leave the two of them alone and do the dishes. From the kitchen, I can hear them talking, but not the words.

Then, after not very long, I notice everything's quiet. I dry my hands on my pants, go back out to the living room where I'd left the two of them on the couch. They're gone.

I walk through the house, down to the basement. It still smells of the cigarettes my father smoked, covertly, when he hid from my mother on the stairs in the dark. I walk past my father's old work clothes, still hanging on a nail, and over to the door leading to the backyard. It's open.

And there they are, the two of them, Dave and my mother in her garden. My mother is standing, hands on hips, chin up, regal, supervising. Dave, hungover, lashless, hater of all vegetables, in button-down plaid shirt and khakis, is on his hands and knees. He's plucking weeds. His hands are filthy. He's sweating. There are mud streaks on his face and shredded weeds in his hair.

"Wild onions," my mother explains as she plops down in a lawn chair. "They choke out everything good I put in."

Dave's job, apparently, is to dig through the garden and pull out every single wild onion bulb. There are hundreds, maybe thousands. They are small and hard and smell stronger than ordinary onions, more gamey.

"Do not do that," I say.

"Mind your own business," my mother says. "He's his own person. He can do what he wants."

Dave waves one muddied hand over his head. "It's fine," he says. "I've got it." He's pale, sweating. I have no idea how he's managed to not throw up.

An hour goes by like this before my mother allows him to stop.

"You didn't get them all," she says, "but you did pretty good."

There are mounds of onion bulbs everywhere, like little graves. Dave looks dizzy. His khakis are scabbed over with patches of mud and fertilizer and smashed weeds. He looks at my mother and nods. He looks at me and blinks his lash-free eyes fast and I wonder if this is code.

When my mother's not looking, he mouths, "What the the fuck?" and shrugs but he is somehow smiling.

We go back in the house. Dave washes up in the bathroom. He's in there a long time and I worry he might be sick, but when he comes out, he looks better than when we left the apartment earlier.

"This one," my mother says as I kiss her goodbye before I get in the car with Dave, "seems o.k."

"Yes," I say.

I'm shocked she hasn't asked more questions, where Dave's living, for instance, or where he'll spend the night.

"This one," she says, "seems pretty good."

"He does," I say.

"I'll call first thing in the morning, so pick up your phone," my mother says. "I have a doctor's appointment. Don't be late."

Out in the car, Dave's waiting. He puts the driver's seat back and rolls down the window. He takes big breaths of onion-free air, in then out.

"She seems happy," he says later as we're driving. "I think she's glad you found someone."

"She wasn't too rough on you?"

"I like her," Dave says. "She reminds me of the old women who used to drink at the dive bars that served me when I was a kid."

"My mom would not think that is a compliment."

"She should."

"Did she praise you for being normal sized?" I ask, and Dave pats my knee. "Many times," he says.

Chapter 36

I suspect for a week I might be pregnant. I have been clinically certain for one day. But even before all this, there were signs. I ignored them because I'm almost middle-aged, because I'm on birth control, because people like me don't just wind up pregnant on accident and Dave and I haven't been together long and it should really take some time for someone like me to get pregnant after all.

"You'll have a hard time getting pregnant," a gynecologist told me years ago. "Your uterus is tipped."

"Tipped?" I said.

I thought about a game football players purportedly did in high school during their down time. Cow tipping. The story was, they'd go into a cow pasture and run full on into the side of a cow and knock it over, poor thing. Of course the football players would be drunk. Of course the cow would be huge and unsuspecting, Of course no one I knew who wasn't on the football team had ever witnessed this.

It was probably impossible, a suburban legend, right up there with Bigfoot and UFOs and my own chances of becoming unexpectedly pregnant.

The gynecologist had explained my uterus this way: "Tipped. Like a rocking chair. It's leaning back. It's common, but it can be a problem when you want to conceive."

I have never been someone who wanted to conceive. I like children, but haven't been around them much, and don't know what to do with them. Gina says that when it comes to children, I have the maternal instincts of a flag pole.

"Not a problem," I said to the gynecologist back then.

And now it was.

<u><></u>

There were early signs.

Lately I wake up before 8 a.m. and blissful without an alarm clock, coffee or National Public Radio.

National Public Radio now seems depressing, while the awful jazz that comes on between segments soothes. Area rugs. I can't resist them. This week I bought three.

I went out for groceries and came back with rugs. The rug in the kitchen is covered in fruit. The rug in the living room is a multi-colored shag that looks like Fruit Loops run through a blender. In the bedroom, the fake sheepskin I love to curl my toes into smells flammable.

Coffee smells like vinegar and toenail clippings. Wine makes me sick. I fall asleep before midnight. I crave, for the first time in a dozen years, steak. Preferably thick. Ideally bloody. I can't get enough orange juice. I drink it straight from the carton when no one's looking.

Then there are the boobs. One night, a few weeks back, I went to sleep as usual, face down, and woke feeling like someone had stuffed two snow globes under my skin. At first I thought it was because my period was late. These were period boobs. My period is often late, nothing unusual there. But then my period still didn't come and the boobs stuck around and kept growing. For the first time in my life, I can fit into a bathing suit. If I bend over and scrunch my shoulders, I can make cleavage. My chest has started to look like something I could put a plate on.

It's terrifying.

"You look great," Dave says one day. Later he says, "Why are your tits suddenly so big?"

But neither of us put it all together at first.

* * *

<>

Now my period's nearly two months late.

"Perimenopause?" Gina says, and I say, "Please," and she says, "But you're old," and I say, "No older than you."

I haven't ever been this late before, and I think it's good to be sure, to rule things out, so I decide to stop by the mall. There's a pharmacy on the lower level, right next to Yankee Candle.

Yankee's scent of the day is Buttercream. I usually love Buttercream, the way it reminds me of birthday cake and frosting, but today it smells fake, like margarine, and makes me nauseous.

In the pharmacy, I have a hard time deciding which pregnancy test to buy. I read all the boxes, then settle on two different packages. Both tests claim to be highly accurate. Both can be used any time of the day. Both are supposed to be easy to read. Plus sign = Pregnant. Minus sign, not pregnant. Color coding is involved, baby pinks and blues.

At the checkout, I hand over the boxes and feel myself blush, as if the girl at the counter, her long hair the color of red devil's food, a star-shaped metal stud through her lip, knows everything about me and would care enough to judge. But she scans the boxes like they're nothing, like they're packs of candy or gum.

"Is that it?" she says, not even looking up, and I say, "That's it."

I don't think I'm pregnant, not really.

I think I am, more likely, dying. I think I've probably come down with some horrible disease, a cancer nestled deep inside my tipped uterus that will kill me within the month.

Still.

I duck into the mall bathroom and rip open the first box of tests. There are two tests per box. I pee on the first stick and try to avoid my fingers. The stick turns pink.

This shows it's working! the package says.

Minutes later, I stare at a blue plus sign. It's blurry, so I do the test again. Second stick. Pink. Blue plus sign. This one is steadier.

I open the second box. I unwrap one of the sticks. Repeat. I hold it very still and stare. The pink washes over the tiny window like a sunset. The plus sign lifts up, like a sky-colored car coming head on in the fog.

All around me, the stall is covered in graffiti. It seems like it should be profound, the way it seems, during a car accident, the dashboard radio should just stop playing. The gravity of an event like this should be enough to knock the airwaves dead and fill up the world with silence.

I catch myself looking for insight in all these messages of love and hate scrawled out in permanent Sharpie markers, the way crazy people look for Jesus in their English muffins.

There isn't much. Snippets of bumper-sticker wisdom – *Keep your rosaries off my ovaries.* Assorted rhymes about pee – *If you sprinkle when you tinkle.* The many incarnations of plus signs – *Cara + Rocco 4EVR.* The many ways to say forever. *4EvOr.*

This is what I'm thinking – forever. I'm thinking about Dave, how I'm going to tell him, how I'll explain this, what I'm, what we're going to do – when a group of teen-aged girls come in. Their heels click on the linoleum. They giggle. A purse unzips. Hairspray cans hiss. Fingers shuffle through makeup bags.

"Give me your lip gloss," one of them says. "I look like I'm fucking dying here."

Chapter 37

"What am I going to do?" I say to Gina when I call hours later.

"What do you mean?" she says. She's chewing something. She goes on chewing. "Congratulations."

I say, "Are you kidding me?"

"Everything happens for a reason. It's the universe's way of telling you something," Gina says, and if she were here, I would punch her.

"Why don't you ask the universe this?" I say. "Ask it what the fuck I'm supposed to do."

"Tell Dave, for one," she says. "There's a start. Just pick the right time. You'll be fine."

I say, "We barely know each other."

"You love him," Gina says. "You're two responsible adults."

"Sure," I say. "We're very responsible for this."

"So," Gina says.

"So what?" I say.

"Don't turn your hormones on me," Gina says.

After I hang up, I convince myself it's a mistake. I take the last pregnancy test out of my bag and rip it open.

In the bathroom, I jiggle it. I hold it up to the light. I look at it from all angles. I hold it still and wait to see if it will change. I will it to change. The plus sign just gets darker, more insistent, urgent. I wrap the stick in a paper towel and carry it back to the bedroom and stash it in my underwear drawer.

Later Dave and I are in bed. It's early, but already he's dozed off.

He had a job interview this afternoon. We found the ad for the job on Monster.com. The job looked perfect on paper – a manager for a bookstore at the airport. He'd make decent money. His unemployment was about to run out and he was running out of savings bonds to cash. It's more expensive than it seems to keep two people living on toast and area rugs. I had thousands in credit card debt I'd built up living in New York, and my landlord had raised the rent $200 because someone, probably Simon next door, had ratted us out.

"At least you're not a woman," my landlord told Dave when she met him. "Women are hell on the plumbing."

"The commute will be awful," he said about the bookstore job, "but I'll be around books."

"The timing couldn't be better," he said.

He said, "It's better than shooting speed at a truck stop."

I helped him do his resume. I helped him practice for his interview. I asked fake questions like "How well do you multi-task?" and "What's your management philosophy?"

"My management philosophy?" he said. "I'll do a good job so I can get a paycheck to pay for bills and rent and booze and come home every night to a beautiful woman I love to fuck and never drive a truck again. How's that?"

I said, "When can you start?"

When he left for the interview, he looked the part of a bookstore manager, from his tie and khakis to his leather satchel. It would help that he was a writer, that he truly loved books. He was always dragging me off to bookstores – City

Books, El Jay's, Barnes & Noble, and his favorite, Caliban. I loved books, too, but he'd spend hours, days scanning the stacks, trying to discover new writers, reconnecting with ones he already knew. I'd never seen anyone so thoughtful.

It took him an hour to get to the airport, an hour and a half to get home in traffic. He'd done well in the interview, and it looked like he'd get the job.

"I don't think she noticed me sweating," he said of Elaine, the woman who interviewed him and would be his boss. "She's a big fat woman with a mustache."

The act of interviewing exhausted him. I'd planned to tell him when he got home, but he looked so tired. Now he is lying here snoring and I can't sleep. I watch him -- his high forehead, the long fully-grown-back eyelashes, the skin around his eyelids shot through with light. I watch him a long time.

The bookstore job is about a future. That's something.

"You're two responsible adults," Gina had said about Dave and me, but it isn't true. We are adults, but we live like people who deny adulthood. We own more books than furniture. We eat toast for dinner. We live in an apartment where the floors, the walls, everything seem about to collapse.

I am better at taking care of my mother than I am at taking care of my own life, and this isn't saying much.

Dave and I have been together two months.

How do you bring a child into that? Why would anyone bring a child into that?

I try to tell myself something romantic and ridiculous and impossible, but every thought fills up with words lifted from a greeting card or a graffiti'd bathroom stall. It has nothing to do with truth.

Dave must have felt me watching, because he wakes up all at once, like he's been pinched.

"Aren't you tired?" he says, and rolls over to hold me. The weight of him makes me feel trapped, suffocated.

"I need to get up," I say, and wriggle free. My feet tangle in the blankets and I nearly fall on my face trying to get out of bed. "I need to show you something."

I could wait. I could time it out more. I could let him rest, but I don't.

I go to the dresser and take out the test. I wasn't sure the plus sign would still show up, but it does. If anything, it is clearer than before, an intersection on a map.

Dave looks groggy, confused. He runs both hands through his hair, again and again, until every hair on his head seems to stand on end.

"I'm pregnant," I say, and he says, "There's no way."

"I thought that, too," I say.

"You're kidding," he says.

"I'm sorry," I say.

"You said you were on birth control," he says.

His face is red, his hair is on end. He looks like he might choke me, and I realize in one terrible moment that I don't know him well enough to be sure he won't.

"I'm sorry," I say. I am still holding the stick in the air between us the way people hold up fingers to feel the direction of the wind.

"Hold on," he says.

Then he gets up and sprints to the bathroom, where he will spend the next 10 minutes throwing up. I toss the stick onto the bed where he's just been, then I pick it back up, walk into the kitchen, and throw it away.

Chapter 38

When Dave finally shuts off the water, when he stops throwing up, when he unlocks the door and comes out, I'm on the couch, curled up as small as I can make myself in one corner.

There's no light on in this room, just the light coming from the half-opened door to the bathroom. The way the doorway looks, lit up like that from behind, seems supernatural, like it's not the door to the bathroom at all, like it leads into another dimension, someplace terrifying and unknown, or someplace wonderful and unknown, both.

Dave sits down beside me. He doesn't say anything. He just sits there.

We sit there, not speaking.

Chapter 39

Dave says, "Do what you think is right." He says, "I'm with you." He says, "We'll be fine, either way." He says, "You choose."

Thinking about choice – to have a baby or not, to keep it or not -- is one thing when you're 20. It's another when you're 35.

I say to Dave, "Help me," and he says, "I can't," and I say, "Please," and he says, "I'm sorry."

He won't say what he wants, what he doesn't want. "I love you," he says, and I say, "I love you, too," and hope that will be enough.

Dave holds me when we sleep, wraps me tight in his arms, one leg thrown around my legs like a vise, but I feel the line between us.

Once, back when I was flying, I was working a red eye, Pittsburgh to Vegas. The pilots called me up to the cockpit to show me a line on the horizon. The line was lit up, orange and white, almost florescent, like a line on a hospital monitor, flat and glowing. Above and below the line, the sky was black, impenetrable, star-less. It's unusual to see this, the pilots said, rarer than the Northern Lights.

"It's the line that separates night from day," one of the pilots explained. "It divides dark from dark."

The line was bright enough to navigate by, a way of keeping the plane's wings level, without instruments, without the tower, without help.

"You choose," Dave says.

I can't even say the word. I can't bear to write it down on the lists I make, pros and cons, options, as if there could be a possibility, as if it might be a choice. It's too painful to even think about, not when I've lost my father, when I could lose my mother.

I can't do any more loss.

I don't know how to tell Dave this. I wait weeks, trying to be sure enough of my own heart that I can translate it to him.

"The line that separates dark from dark," the pilot said. Something steady and powerful enough to divide the sky.

I never thought I'd be a mother. I never could have imagined myself as a mother. I don't think Dave's ever seen himself as a father. I know he never imagined himself married.

"I swore I'd never be with someone just to be with them," he told me. "I knew I had to have everything in common with a person. I'm fine alone. I like being alone."

I've been fine alone, too, and now I'm not.

Some women know early on they want to have children. I've never been like that. It's not that I can't imagine having a family. It's that I've never been able to imagine being that connected to anyone.

I know a lot of adopted people who blame all their problems on that initial loss. "It never heals," my friend Janice says. She and I were adopted from the same orphanage. She's 12 years older than me, has never had kids, still dresses in a black leather jacket and nose rings, still plays at being a child. "People think we're fine," she says, "but really, there's no coming back."

I never believed that. But still, this idea of having a physical and emotional connection, a biological link, is foreign to me. It will be years before I will meet anyone from my biological family. Right now, pregnant and frightened, I've never seen anyone who looked like me or shared my DNA.

Although I've always known my parents loved me, there has always been a vague sense of something missing, even if it's just that we look nothing alike.

I'm blonde. My father had dark hair. My mother did, too, before it went grey. I'm tall. They're short. It doesn't seem like it should matter much, but somehow it does.

When I was very young, my mother used to make us matching outfits. They were pretty outfits – black velvet dresses, gold lame suits, apricot scooter skirts. When we'd go out to the mall, the bank, or the grocery, I knew it meant a lot to her for people to stop and say, "You two look like twins" or, "She has your eyes."

A nice cardigan-wearing therapist told me once that there is a list of classic symptoms – separation anxiety, intimacy issues, fear of abandonment, fear of powerlessness – that are common for adoptees. Some of them seemed familiar.

"It may explain the intensity of your relationship with your mother, your fear of losing her," he said. "It may explain a lot of things." And then he gave me a stack of self-help books to read.

"You want to get better," my mother would say, "help yourself."

I'm thinking about airplanes again, how my happiest moments were when the wheels lifted off the ground and I was separated from everything and everyone I knew. I was happiest with my life in a suitcase, with nothing to make me hold still. I don't have friends from kindergarten. Aside from Gina, I don't have friends from college. The only reason Gina and I are still friends is because she's refused to let me go. I don't call my aunts on their birthdays. I don't have friendly relationships with my exes. In the family plot at Braddock Cemetery, the space next to my parents' plot belongs to a cousin. There's no space for me. I didn't choose this, but if someone had asked me, I would have.

"Adopted people," the nice therapist said, "are afraid of being invisible, so sometimes they make themselves invisible."

Once, years from now, drunk, I will explain it to Dave this way:

"I never thought anything I ever did could matter much to anyone. I barely even exist."

It will be drunk, melodramatic nonsense.

It will be one of the truest things I'll ever say.

But now I don't have the luxury, the self-indulgence to think these things. And besides, those things, if they'd been true once, if they'll be true later, weren't true now. There is this other person inside me. Not a fetus. A person. There's Dave. I can't escape, and I don't think I want to.

I've already been having lucid dreams. Pregnant women, I've read, often have these. They're vivid, in color, and I remember them when I don't remember many other things.

In the dreams, I meet my son. He has Dave's sweet round face and he's built solid, like a pork-chop. But he's blonde, like me, and he has my green eyes, which isn't fair, since his father's eyes are the most beautiful blue I've ever seen. But it's my son's hands I focus on most. They're big, long-fingered. They look like starfish.

Years from now, I'll find my birth family. When we meet, my sister will ask me to hold up my hands. She'll press her palms to mine, and my brother will fold his hands over ours, measuring. We know each other by our hands.

In the dream, my son's hands are busy. They're throwing things. Clothes, mostly. He stands inside a suitcase and tosses everything out. He laughs and throws and makes a huge mess. When he's done, he looks right at me, like he's going to say something, but he doesn't.

It doesn't matter. I know what he means.

I'm not going anywhere.

Chapter 40

And so we are going to have a baby. The doctors confirm it. Dave and I go together to the appointments. My face is pale. Dave's face is red, he sweats. I try not to be sick even though everything in me feels like I'm bobbing on an inner tube at sea, moving further and further from anything that looks like land.

The first doctor, a boy-faced man in pleated polyester pants and a Bugs Bunny tie, asks, "And how are you going to decorate the nursery?"

The second one says, "Congratulations, mom and dad!"

No one seems to think about the possibility that we hadn't planned this.

We look like what Gina said we are, responsible adults. We pass. There are blood tests, weekly appointments, and countless exams.

"Do you want a boy or a girl?" a kind nurse asks, then stops herself. "As long as it's healthy, right?"

She says, "Congratulations."

She says, "Is this your first?"

"I feel like a fraud," Dave says.

"That's not the right word for it," I say, but I don't have a better word.

Chapter 41

We drive to Michigan so I can meet Dave's parents. Their house is beautiful, one in a series of beautiful houses in a subdivision outside of Detroit. The Detroit I've seen is rundown, dangerous, all those houses with windows punched out like teeth. This is not that Detroit. There's a mall and a bagel shop nearby. There are bird feeders in the yard and wind-chimes in the trees and a collection of plates with inspirational sayings on them scattered on shelves throughout the house. Every room smells like cinnamon and peaches. When the wind blows, the house fills up with the soft ting of chimes.

Dave's father is an autoworker. His mother does hearing and visions tests for kids in inner city schools. They're nice. They're so nice I feel ashamed keeping secrets from them.

"We can tell them later. Let's wait a while," Dave says. It's what I say when it comes to my mother, too. Eventually I'll start showing, and then that will be that. Until then, there doesn't seem to be reason to upset things.

Dave's mother is beautiful, with blonde hair and green eyes. His dad is from the Bronx and his eyes are as blue as his son's. He and I talk a lot about New York, how much we both love it. He tells me stories about his days in the merchant marines. He tells me about his time in Spain.

"He's never told me those stories," Dave says, and I say, "Never? In all those years you were growing up?" and Dave says, "He didn't talk to me." "Why not?" I say. Dave says, "He worked awful jobs. You don't feel like talking when you come home from awful jobs."

Dave's mother makes a chocolate trifle and serves it in crystal bowls. Everyone is polite and kind. Neither of his parents asks us anything personal, not even where Dave lives.

"It is so lovely to meet you," his mother says. "Dave never brings girls home."

Her skin glistens pink, like the inside of a sea shell. She has a slight accent. "Hillbilly," Dave says, joking, because she's from West Virginia.

"Genteel," I say, which I think is exactly the right word.

Chapter 42

We all get along. Dave's parents and I, my mother and Dave, my mother and I.

The doctors say my mother is doing well, much better than expected. "You can't kill me," she says to the doctor with the nice hands who still seems afraid of her.

Dave has gotten his bookstore job. The hours and the commute are awful – he's up at 5 a.m., not home until 6 p.m. – but he thinks it will get better. He likes being around books. There's a Godiva store next to the bookstore and the manager sells him the old chocolates for pennies and Dave brings home truffles in a tiny gold bag.

It's a strangely peaceful time. When I'm not worrying, when I'm not thinking too much, I'm happy.

Dave and I don't mention I'm pregnant to anyone. We don't mention we live together, even though it's obvious. We don't mention his cashed-in savings bonds, the sagging apartment. We don't lie to anyone or ourselves, but we don't tell the truth about anything, either.

"Have you thought about baby names?" the kind nurse asks me, and I tell her I haven't.

Chapter 43

My mother and I are at her kitchen table. We clip coupons. There are little piles everywhere. If one of us sneezes, it would destroy my mother's elaborate sorting system which divides the coupons into product types, expiration dates and, in descending order, amounts off.

This system never works. I often find myself in the grocery, swearing under my breath as I riffle through my mother's coupon-keeper, where I'll eventually find a must-have coupon for chocolate chips filed under Personal Hygiene.

It has been nearly two months since doctors confirmed I was pregnant. I'm starting to look like I've swallowed a Bundt cake, and my mother has started to lecture about eating habits.

"You have to eat to live and not live to eat," she says.

"Ask yourself," she says, "do I really need another cookie?"

"Try on these pants," she says, holding up a hot-pink polyester pair with an elastic waist. "They're too big for me, but I bet they'll fit you."

"Maybe you should tell her," I say to Dave. "She likes you better."

"You'll find the right time. I support whatever you do," he says, trying to be funny. He supports whatever I do, I'm realizing, because he's avoided contact his whole life. He doesn't seem to care what anyone thinks. I know this applies to other people, his parents, even. I'm not sure how much it applies to me. He's always lived in tiny apartments away from the world, and then the back of a truck, distant from connection. He seems to like almost everyone, but he never invites anyone around.

Dave's at the computer, writing. He doesn't even look up. These days, every minute is filled, and because it's summer, because I'm off from teaching, because I'm worried and nauseous and completely hormonally not myself, I'm often furious. Dave's working at the bookstore, long awful days. He tries to write when he can -- on weekends, late at night, when he has to be up with the sun.

His mustached boss, Elaine, is, as he'd guessed from his interview, awful. She calls him in to work on his days off. She waits until five minutes before he's supposed to punch out to tell him she needs him to do overtime. There's always urgent paperwork, huge piles of it, whenever he's about to go home.

"You have to have priorities," she says.

She says, "Are you committed to this company?"

"I need you to be a team player," she says. "Your home life can wait."

Elaine, unlike our families, knows I'm pregnant.

"Don't even think," she says to Dave early on, "about using your wife's pregnancy as an excuse."

Dave's making $30,000 a year for this. "Just quit," I say, but we both know he can't.

One day, a few weeks back, after he'd done 15 days straight and needed sleep, Dave called in to work. He said he'd been in a car accident. He said he was fine, but was going to the hospital to get checked out. He was afraid Elaine wouldn't believe him. He was probably right. She wouldn't believe him. She'd need police reports, insurance documents. She'd need to inspect the car.

And so he went into the bathroom with a serrated bread knife. I didn't know why. When he came back out, his forehead was scratched and gouged raw. He was bleeding.

"I hit my head on the windshield," he said, smiling, pointing at his forehead. "How does it look?"

I said, "Bad."

And then he went back to bed, relieved, and bled all over the pillows.

This is how desperate things were getting, and the baby wasn't even here yet.

"How's the nursery coming?" the one doctor with the cartoon ties keeps asking. His voice is perky as alka-seltzer. His hair is sharp, gelled into neat little spikes. He looks and sounds like a Muppet.

"We're going with a Winnie-the-Pooh theme," I say. "That way we're good for a boy or a girl."

In our train-car apartment, of course, there is no nursery. The baby would share a room with our computers, the room where I'd once stashed George's stinky chair. Dave and I would keep trying to write between naps, at least until the landlord found out and had us all evicted. If she thought women were hard on plumbing, I knew what she'd think about children.

"Children," she'd say, "destroy everything."

Which is what I am about to do to my mother. At least that's how I feel, sitting here with the coupon piles, a pair of safety scissors in one hand and a newspaper insert in the other, waiting for the right moment to tell her I am not eating myself to death and that she is going to be a grandmother instead.

I try to convince myself she'll be happy. She has probably given up on any hopes of me having children, and so this is, quite possibly, a miracle. She likes Dave. She carries pictures of her monosyllabically-named friends' grandchildren in her wallet and may, for all I know, be passing the cutest ones off as her own. There are a lot of cute puffy-paint sweatshirts made especially for The World's Best Grandmothers. Maybe, somehow, the prospect of a grandchild will become something joyous for her, like picking the right door on "The Price is Right" or beating me at "Jeopardy."

"Here," my mother says, pushing a pile of tampon coupons at me. "Make sure you use them. Every penny counts, you know."

I push the pile back and take a breath. "No thanks," I say.

"They add up," she says. "You'd be amazed."

"I know," I say. "But I don't need them."

"You think you're too good to use coupons?" she says.

"No," I say. "I'm saying I don't need them. The tampons, I mean."

I say, "I need you to be calm. Don't get upset."

I say, "It's not good for you to be upset."

I say, "I'm pregnant."

My mother stops sorting. She puts down the scissors, as if her hands can't be trusted with them. She looks at me over the rims of her oversized reading glasses.

"What did you say?" she says.

"I'm pregnant," I say.

"No you're not," she says, and I smile, pat her hand, smile more. "Yes," I say, "I am."

She does not smile back. She takes off her glasses. She glares as if I've run out in traffic and forced her to slam the brakes.

"That's impossible," she says, each syllable a scissor snip. "You can't be. You're not married."

"That really has nothing to do with it," I say.

Her hands splay flat on the table, bracing. When she was young, when I was a child, she was a slapper. The slap would come when I wasn't suspecting it. It would land hard across my face, my arm, anywhere she could reach.

I stare at my mother and try to guess her move. I try not to flinch.

"It has everything to do with it," she says, and keeps her hands in place.

"I'm in love, I'm pregnant, I'm happy," I say.

"Get married," she says.

"No," I say.

"Now," she says.

"When we're ready," I say.

And then she says it. "I didn't know I had a whore for a daughter."

"I'm middle-aged," I say.

"Then you should know better," she says. "You will get married. What will people think? I will not have this. Do you understand me? I will not have this."

The sick woman, the woman with the bad heart, the woman with cancer and heartbreak, is gone. The woman here in front of me, her hands balling now into fists, is fierce and strong and everything about her is a weapon.

I stand up. "I'll call you later," I say, and she says, "Don't bother until you make this right."

On my way out, I stop, turn back. She's still sitting at the table, frozen in her anger. "I hoped you'd be happy," I say. "I really thought you'd be happy."

"Why would you think that?" she says.

Chapter 44

I want my mother and everyone in this to be happy because I know now that, despite everything, I'm happy. I'm happy even as I drive away from my mother's pink-bricked house and onion-free garden. I'm happy sitting in traffic. I'm happy when I drive past Miracle Mile Shopping Center and a garbage truck cuts me off and the sun beams down and I have to squint because I've forgotten my sunglasses on my mother's kitchen table next to a pile of coupons, all those cents-off promises that life can somehow be managed, balanced like a checkbook.

I think of my son, the way he shows up in my dreams. I don't know yet from the doctors that I'm having a boy, but I am, and he will look exactly the way he does in those dreams, his hands will be exactly like mine, and there will be no explaining any of it.

My hands now are on the steering wheel, at 10 o'clock and 2 o'clock, just like my father taught me, safe and steady and in control.

I'm happy thinking about Dave trying to find the right words in the glare of his computer screen. I'm happy thinking about his beautiful tired face, the desperate cuts on his forehead healed over. I'm happy thinking that someday we'll do better, someday we'll make this work and be writers and parents and drink wine and maybe even sleep a little.

I'm happy even though I'm terrified, even though happiness, in life like in books, is neither logical nor likely. This is why the word happy doesn't often show up in literature.

When a national bookstore interviewed a group of American writers about the most overused word in American literature, not one of them put the word "happy" on the list. "It's petunia," Brad Land says. "It's everywhere." For Augusten Burroughs, it's "frottage." I had to look that one up. It's what people do when they make charcoal rubbings of tombstones. It's also a euphemism for dry humping. No one's asked me, but if they did, I'd probably say something tacky like "scrotum," then blame it on Tourette's or banned children's books. Some writers, some people, love to be clever and show off. We love to find humor in everything because life is pretty scary otherwise.

"Everything's a joke to you," my father used to tell me. It was true and it wasn't true.

If I were going to be serious about this word thing, though, I'd agree with Alan Gratz. It really is "suddenly." Suddenly – a word that's as tough to hold back as a hiccup, even though every writer knows it's a bargain-basement way to make an awkward transition, to explain what can't be explained.

As in: and then, suddenly, everything changed.

Chapter 45

Before I moved home to Pittsburgh, I went to see that nice therapist in New York, the one who filled me in on my adoption issues. I went on the advice of my friend Meg, who, even though she believes we are all essentially alone in the world, is a very good friend. She's also a native New Yorker, neurotic, sad. She's been seeing therapists for years.

Meg sees more therapists than movies. Every Christmas, when she's feeling down, she checks herself into an exclusive hospital that offers private rooms, tai chi, aromatherapy and massage. Many of Meg's fellow patients are celebrities and she always brings back great gossip: the famous author/sex addict; the rock star who eats lipstick; the anorexic celebrity chef.

"They're all nuts," Meg says.

Meg isn't nuts, at least I don't think so. She has a hard time navigating the world, like many people, but unlike many people, she's rich. Her mother died when Meg was very young Her mother was a painter and had known DeKooning. Meg's family had summered in the Hamptons. Her mother had been lovely. She adored pin stripes and the color blue and Meg loved her very much.

Now, decades later, Meg's father is old and alone. When he doesn't answer his phone, when he goes out for a sandwich or takes the subway downtown without telling her, Meg believes he's dead. She calls the building superintendent. She calls the police and ambulance. One day she called me. I went with her to her father's building. When he wouldn't answer the buzzer, when no one would buzz us in, I pulled down the rusty fire escape and climbed up while Meg sat weeping on the stairs.

Her father lives on the fifth floor. It was a rough climb, and I thought some of the stairs might crumble, they were that rusted out, unused. "It's o.k.," I kept saying to Meg. "I'm sure he's fine."

But what did I know? I wasn't even sure when I was trying to pry open a window that it was her father's window and not someone else's, someone who might be disturbed by the thought of a grown woman in black tights and combat boots trying to force her way into a stranger's kitchen.

Just when I got the window loose, just after I was dive bombed by some pigeons that had been nesting on the overhang of a dripping air conditioner, Meg's father came home. He had a sandwich in a brown paper bag. He had the Times rolled up under his arm.

"What the hell are you people doing?" he said.

Meg believed everyone would leave her, and because she believed this, they often did.

I haven't seen Meg in a few years. I went to see this therapist she recommended just once. I went because I was worried about coming home. I was worried about how I would deal with my mother. I was, as they say in therapy-speak, trying to come to terms with things.

The therapist was a nice man. He did not have a beard and looked nothing like Freud. He wore a cardigan and penny loafers and reminded me of Mr. Rogers, but without the puppets. His office was in the same building as a bowling alley. The building had an ancient elevator and an elevator man who wore a cap and hand-cranked the elevator's steel cage door shut. The elevator looked dangerous and sturdy all at once.

Inside the therapist's office, I expected to hear the sounds of crashing pins, the grind of the elevator making its way up and down the spine of the building, but the only sounds were peaceful, echoes of traffic, a hint of canned classical music wafting in from the waiting room. All around, there were strategically-placed boxes of tissue. There were watercolors and fresh flowers and the office smelled like nutmeg and mildew.

"Are you comfortable?" the therapist asked. He said, "Please. Make yourself at home," as if I'd dropped in for a visit, as if I'd come by for tea.

The bowling alley was a few floors down. Most of the people I knew back home in Pittsburgh wouldn't understand my friend Meg or a bowling alley in a skyscraper any more than they'd understand why I'd pay money to talk to a stranger about my mother. They'd say bowling – the art of flinging something heavy in order to knock down other equally heavy things – is therapy enough.

During that one session, the therapist suggested, in addition to those self-help books, journaling. He suggested yoga and told me to make lists.

"Lists give you a sense of order and control," he said. "You're a writer. So write it down. What do you want? What would you say to your mother if you weren't afraid to say it?"

The advice seemed simple and reasonable. I was glad my insurance had covered most of the visit.

"It's common sense," I said to Meg. "People pay for that?"

"You'd be surprised," she said.

Still, when Dave was merging and re-arranging our books, I found an anthology of bar poems I'd been reading back around that time. I opened the book and there, scribbled inside the front and back covers, was a list, all these words lined up like bowling pins.

I'd written, "I love you." I'd written, "I'm afraid you'll die." I'd written, "I don't want to lose you" and "I don't want to get lost." I'd written, "I want you to be happy" and, next to that, "I want to be happy." I'd written, "I want this to be my choice."

Chapter 46

The airline's "Marry Me, Fly Free" shirts were funny and humiliating and possibly desperate, but many new flight attendants wore them. The shirts got a lot of attention in hotel bars. Drunk people all over the world take t-shirt advertising very seriously.

"This shirt's better than a dating service," my friend Carrie used to say. Carrie's "Marry Me" t-shirt was tight and lime green. She wore it on layovers and never paid for drinks. "You'd be amazed what people will do for free plane tickets," she'd say.

I'm amazed what people will do for love.

When I finally ask Dave to marry me – not because my mother wants it, but because I want it and hope Dave does, too -- it comes almost out of nowhere. We'd gone out to eat at a restaurant called the Red Star. The Red Star is half restaurant, half train station. The décor is circus kitsch. Above the bar, there are two huge papier-mâché sculptures. The sculptures are two bulbous tightrope walkers, a man and a woman. The walkers are balanced overhead on chubby tiptoe, perched like fat birds on their tightrope, toddling there, against the odds of gravity, against any good sense.

"I have healthcare." This is how I propose, over a plate of potato skins and some peel-and-eat shrimp. "I still have flight benefits."

Dave hates to fly, but he still says yes.

"That was the nicest thing anyone has ever asked me," Dave says later.

"That's the scariest thing I've ever asked," I say.

We don't tell my mother or our friends. We don't call Dave's kind and lovely parents. That weekend, we cash in the last of his savings bonds, buy two simple rings at The Clark Building in Pittsburgh, and fly to Las Vegas for free, first class.

How I know Dave loves me: he said yes, even though both of us had at one point sworn off marriage. And he's not complaining about the flight, even though he's gripping his armrests and sweating so much a flight attendant thinks he might be having a heart attack.

"We're getting married," I say.

"That explains things," she says, and brings us a bottle of champagne and an extra airsickness bag, just in case.

"Close your eyes," I say to Dave. "I'll wake you when we get there."

"I can't sleep up here," he says. "This plane is three sizes too small." He goes to the bathroom and takes more pills.
He tries to read William Carlos William and his sweat drips on the page.

As much as Dave's miserable, I love it up here. After years of working flights like this one, I can sleep better on an airplane than I can at home. Some flight attendants I worked with used to take home recordings of jet engines and play them as white noise so they could sleep on the ground. Dave's more like most people, who think, rightfully so, that flying isn't natural. But I'm with the little old lady who, on a flight to Kansas City once, in the middle of a bad bout of turbulence, threw her arms up and yelled, "They should charge extra for this!"

The flight from Pittsburgh to Vegas, with a stop in Atlanta, takes about six and a half hours. When the plane finally starts to descend, I nudge Dave, who's closed his eyes despite himself, and say, "Look. It's beautiful. Trust me."

Chapter 47

It's around midnight, Vegas time. Flying into Vegas at night is a magical thing. At first there's only desert, one long stretch of black, and then there's light. The signs that make up the Vegas skyline appear and the whole place looks like luck, something invented to sell on TV. On one end of the strip, there's a sphinx and a pyramid. Farther down, there's the Empire State Building and the Brooklyn Bridge, King Arthur's castle and a pirate ship. Vegas looks like the world tossed in a Yahtzee cup. It looks like a jumbled Atlantis rising out of the sea.

"The whole damn place is a dream," my father who loved and believed in Vegas used to say.

"I don't need to go to Paris," a passenger told me once. "I can visit the Eiffel Tower right here, where people speak English."

"Everything's fake," another passenger said, "but it's nicer than the real thing."

I'd wanted to get married in Key West. Key West is literary and romantic. Hemingway had a house there. The descendants of his cats live there still. Tennessee Williams wrote "A Streetcar Named Desire" at the La Concha Hotel. Key West has beautiful sunsets. People get married barefoot on the beach, with the sun breaking open like an egg.

Key West would have been a perfect place for Dave and me to get married. It also seemed more legitimate than Vegas. Vegas is the place where drunk celebrities get married and divorced in 48 hours or less. Vegas is, like my passenger said, fake, which meant getting married in Vegas might be fake, too.

But Vegas it is, because we're broke. Vegas is cheap and uncomplicated. "It doesn't matter where we go," Dave says. "We're not the kind of people who care about those things."

And I think: *we*—even though I was the one to propose. Marriage, and all the possible disasters that can come with it, still seems terrifying. I can't name one couple who calls themselves *we* that likes, let alone loves, each other. Nearly every married couple I know is on their way to divorce or permanent misery. Most *we* couples talk to each other like Day Planners. "It's Tuesday. Don't forget to take out the trash." "The dry cleaners close at 8." "You didn't forget to buy milk, did you?" "I penciled you in for sex a week from Friday."

But we're not those people. We – Dave and I -- are not those people. I roll the thought over and over until I'm sure it's true.

"Isn't it pretty to think so," Hemingway's Jake Barnes echoes back.

Chapter 48

In Vegas, we get a room for $30 a night at Circus/Circus. The hotel is one giant Big Top. The Red Star's papier-mâché trapeze artists feel like foreshadowing. Here there are real trapeze artists. There are mimes and clowns. The concierge is dressed like a circus barker. Being inside Circus/Circus is like being trapped inside a Fellini film. It's like being stuck in a giant pinball machine.

When the writers Tess Gallagher and Ray Carver got married in Nevada's Heart of Reno Chapel, Carver called it a "high tack affair." After the ceremony, Tess went on a three-day winning streak at roulette.

"It's perfect," I say to Dave as we stand in line to check in.

"What?" he says. The bells from the slot machines, the circus music, the crowds – everything except the mimes – drown everything out.

Upstairs in our room, the mattress sags. There are cigarette burns in one pillowcase. A Styrofoam take-out container is moldering under the bed.

"It's not the honeymoon suite," I say.

"Shut up," Dave says, and runs at me full on, knocking me onto the bed that creaks and bows and threatens to snap under our weight.

Later, we hire a cab driver to take us for a tour of wedding chapels. The cabbie, a middle-aged woman in a bedazzled tank top, says she'll look out for us. "A nice couple like you," she says. "I'll get you a big discount."

We drive down the Strip. Howie Mandel is playing the Tropicana. Sinbad is at the MGM. The cabbie seems nice at first. Then she starts talking.

"You picked the perfect place to get married. Vegas is the most romantic place on earth," she says. "Just look at that."

She points to a blonde man and woman on the sidewalk. They are both very tan and dressed in matching white polo shirts. They're holding hands. They look like an ad for a timeshare.

"Now there's a nice couple," she says.

She says, "Not like all these white girls with the black men."

She says, "And those Mexicans. They're everywhere. They're taking over. Just look around."

She says, "We should shoot them all."

I feel sick. We get out of the cab at the next chapel and walk what seems miles back to the hotel. The heat is unbelievable, well over a hundred degrees. Dave is sweating, dry heat or not. I'm dizzy. My tongue swells.

"Fucking psychotic," Dave says about the cab driver.

"I think I might throw up," I say.

But it's more than the cabbie, more than the heat. The whole place seems off, wrong, an illusion. In the hotel lobby, a mime is stuck in an invisible box. A woman dressed in flammable Lycra eats fire. Blindfolded trapeze artists swing overhead and throw themselves at each other. Trust is one thing. The huge net under the high wires is another. Families with children are everywhere. None of them look happy. Most of the children are crying.

I am having a child. I am getting married. All of this is making me sick.

Just off to our right, a couple and their young son are checking in. The son has his own suitcase, a Thomas the Train roller-board. He whacks it back and forth against a marble pillar. His mother says, loud enough for me to hear it over the big-top noise, "Stop it, Tommy."

I think Tommy, Thomas. Cute.

"Tommy, I mean it," the mother says. Her voice is flat as cardboard. She wears sunglasses, celebrity-style frames, black plastic with rhinestone lion-heads at the temples.

The husband drags another suitcase. This one's huge, big enough to store a body in. The check-in line moves like an old movie reel, but the husband stops for a second because the bag's toppled over. He struggles to right it. He doesn't see the girl at the desk who motions him down. He doesn't hear her say, "Next."

The wife hears.

The wife's wearing boots, high heels, black, shiny, sturdy. She kicks once, hard, to get him moving.

The husband barely flinches. He drags the suitcase up to the desk. Tommy drags his Thomas bag too. Tommy's crying. The girl behind the desk gives him a sucker. "Stop it, Tommy," the mother says, and Tommy goes on crying.

People get married and have children and do unbelievable, hideous things to each other.

Dave is red faced, his shirt soaked. He flops into a chair. I bring him a bottle of water I buy from the front desk cooler for five dollars. I say, "Maybe we should go home." He gulps the water down in one long chug. I watch his Adam's apple move up and down beneath the soft skin of his throat.

"We came all this way," he says when he finally comes up for air.

That night, when Dave falls asleep, I flip through channels. I watch reruns of "The X Files," where the poster in Fox Mulder's office never changes. It's a picture of a flying saucer coming in for a landing in some suburb. There are trees and well-groomed lawns and pretty little houses with families inside. The poster says, "I Want to Believe."

We get married the next night at The Special Memory Wedding Chapel on the Strip. It's an all-white building with a gazebo and a bell tower and a flashing neon sign that advertises drive-through wedding service. We opt for the regular walk down the aisle.

If we had the money, we could be married by an impersonator called Elvis the Pelvis Himselvis. Grandpa Munster could give me away. We could get commemorative t-shirts with our faces and the words "Making Special Memories Together" on them.

As it is, Dave wears his own plain white t-shirt. He pins a rose on the pocket. I wear a lilac dress I ordered from the Spiegel catalogue. I carry the tiny bouquet that comes with our Bargain Memory package. We are married by a tall Unitarian minister who looks like he plays a Unitarian minister on TV. He talks about love being patient and kind. He talks about how some marriages work and some don't. He shrugs, then talks about honesty and trust. His $50 suggested tip is mandatory and included on our bill.

On the wedding video, I blink a lot. I blink when I'm nervous. I look like someone squirted vinegar in my eyes. Dave's face shines. His cheeks are red. He smiles and beams. The only time I stop blinking and he stops beaming is when we kiss. In that moment, preserved forever on tape in case we ever doubt it, we both look calm and certain, sure of the world and our place in it.

When we turn to leave, our one witness, the chapel receptionist, is clapping. She's bored. She's probably done this all day. She claps, slow and polite. She claps like an audience that's happy the show's finally over. The clapping bounces off the walls of the empty chapel. The neon drive-through sign flashes overhead. Off to the right, there's a gift shop with t-shirts and postcards and Special Memory refrigerator magnets shaped like doves.

Right before the camera pans out, Dave does a cheer. He kicks his left leg. He punches the air with both fists. The camera zooms in and it's just the two of us. I lean into him and we walk off together like that. It looks perfect. It looks like forever.

Chapter 49

There's opera on the stereo. The music is too big for Aunt Thelma's white-and-yellow sided house, which used to be my grandmother's white-and-yellow sided house, a house that looks like a duck with a yellow-bricked porch for a beak. The music's too big for Aunt Thelma's stereo, which used to be my grandmother's stereo, actually a record player with two crackly speakers, a penny taped to the arm just over the needle to keep it from skipping.

I don't know much about opera, but I recognize Mario Lanza, "the world's most romantic tenor," critics called him. He's Aunt Thelma's and my mother's favorite. Neither my mother nor my aunt love opera. They've never been to the opera. They love Mario Lanza because he's Italian, because he's handsome, and because he's from Philadelphia, which is close enough to call home.

Mario Lanza wasn't born Mario Lanza. He changed his name from Alfred Arnold Cocozza to match his mother's name. Her name was Maria Lanza. He loved her very much.

"You did what?" my mother is saying. She has to raise her voice over Mario's, which is a feat now that he's transitioned into "Ave Maria."

"A voice like angel wings," Aunt Thelma says, one finger in the air, conducting.

I know this song. My father used to sing it in church.

My mother's face is flushed. She wears a necklace I gave her a few years back. The necklace is fancy, fit for the opera, fit for church, a purple-flowered choker with rhinestones on all the petals. Her neck muscles flex and strain against the chain. I think I can see her pulse. She looks like she's actually choking.

We've been invited for dinner, my mother, Dave and me. Pasta, meatballs, red wine. Garlic wafts like fog over everything. We're in the living room. My mother is in an overstuffed velvet chair, directly across from where Dave and I sit close together on the couch. The couch cushions smell like onions. A heightened sense of smell is one of the symptoms of pregnancy. I've been reading up.

My mother sits with her feet flat on the floor, her back straight, her chin level with her shoulders. She looks regal and joyless. She looks like a statue from ancient Rome. Mario's winged voice lifts, vibrates the curtains. I want to tell my mother again she's only half Italian, so she should knock it off.

She's been scowling like a mob boss ever since Aunt Thelma, who didn't know I was pregnant, who thought I'd just chunked up, poured two glasses of wine and set them in front of Dave and me. My mother waited to see if I dare take a sip. She glared at the glasses and at me like she wanted to shatter us both.

Dave and I have been home for a week. We haven't told our families we're married, but we did call a few friends. We got everyone together to celebrate at a restaurant called The Pleasure Bar in Bloomfield. For years, I thought The Pleasure Bar was a strip club, but it's really a family-style Italian restaurant. There are fake grapevines on the walls and old wax-dripped Chianti-bottle candlesticks on the tables.

Gina came, and June and Ed, Bobby and Amy. Our army-vet-turned-artist friend Shane came, too. He showed up in a scarf and Jackie O sunglasses, his red afro held back with a headband. When the waitress asked him what he'd like to drink, Shane said "vodka." When the waitress said, "a double?" Shane said, "at least."

Shane took pictures he'd send along months later, the usual wedding-reception shots, along with other pictures – a few strange and well-endowed naked men sleeping, a bowl of fruit, one self portrait of Shane doing the hula, a toilet seat lei around his neck.

Other friends had come from New York – my poet-friends Ann and Frank, flight attendant friends like Brooke. Brooke was still flying. She brought gifts she'd gathered on layovers -- wineglasses from her last trip to Dublin, some white tulip bulbs from Amsterdam. "To plant in your yard," she said, "so you'll have tulips on your anniversary."

I hugged Brooke and said, "I love you. They're perfect. We don't have a yard; we have a fire escape."

"Someday you'll have a yard," she said. "In the meantime, they'll keep."

Everything was like that – happy, hopeful – which may have been why, where my mother was concerned, I was holding onto this latest secret as long as I could.

"You didn't tell her you got married?" Gina said.

"I'm waiting for the right time," I said.

"Oh I'm sure that's a plan," Gina said.

And now here we are at Aunt Thelma's, with Mario Lanza on the stereo, a tray of meatballs in the oven and a nice red sauce bubbling on the stove. Even if it isn't exactly the right time, at least it seems safe. After all, Aunt Thelma is nice, a good buffer.

"So tell us all about your marvelous vacation," Aunt Thelma is saying. "How was it?"

"We went to Vegas," I say. "Just for a few days."

"I love Vegas," Aunt Thelma says, and claps her hands together once to show how much she loves it. "The champagne brunch, the buffets, all that shrimp. Vegas is perfect. I'd like to live in Vegas before I die."

Dave isn't speaking. He looks the way he looked on the plane. Claustrophobic. Crammed in. Stuck. I tuck one foot behind his leg like I'm trying to tie us together, like we're about to tandem skydive with just one parachute we're not sure will work.

"We have some news," I say.

I hold up my left hand, which I've been keeping tucked in a pocket or under my thigh. I look at Dave. We raise our eyebrows, all vaudeville now as Mario, who used to be Alfred, launches into something huge, from La Boheme maybe. Now it's not just the curtains, but it's the paintings on the walls, too – all puzzles of landscapes and farm animals Aunt Thelma's put together, shellacked and framed – that seem to shake. Dave and I fake surprise, try to make this all a joke.

My mother isn't joking. She's not smiling. She's not even blinking. It's as if all that staring has worked. I break into shards.

My mother says, "What are you trying to say?"

Mario Lanza, who was supposed to be one of the world's greatest voices, the next Caruso, watched his career go from critical acclaim in "Madame Butterfly" to being a roadshow for Coca-Cola. He died young, 38, a pulmonary embolism, a bad heart.

I feel my own heart, my pulse in my ears. I look at my mother to see just how worked up she's getting too. It's impossible to tell because she hasn't moved.

"We're married," Dave says, "to each other."

"Oh that's wonderful!" Aunt Thelma says and she claps again. She stomps a foot. "Let's have a toast."

We all pick up a glass, except for my mother. She waits until Thelma nudges her. She waits until Thelma raises her glass over her head like a torch and says, "Bertie! Toast!"

My mother picks up her glass with two fingers, the way she'd hold a snake by the head to keep it from biting. I raise mine. My mother glares. Now I glare back and think, enough.

I clink Dave, clink Aunt Thelma. I raise my glass to my mother, who looks like a tragic figure now, all that anger perched like a vulture on the crystal rim of her wine glass. She would light me on fire if she could.

Mario Lanza launches into "That's Amore," a real crowd-pleasing pop song, the moon like a big pizza pie.

Mario Lanza was not born Mario Lanza.

There's only so much a child can change for a mother.

There are only so many ways to reinvent yourself before you have to own your life.

I mean to fake-sip the wine, then I don't.

Chapter 50

When I was six years old, I played a dog in a musical skit at Sugar Camp Day Camp in Pitcairn, Pennsylvania. My hair was long, perfect for pigtailed dog ears. The camp counselors taped a macramé tail to my shorts and painted a shiny black dog nose on my face.

I thought I looked very smart. I barked and romped on all fours. Then, in front of my fellow campers and their families, I ate a whole Milk Bone. It was green. It didn't taste that bad.

When I padded over to my mother, tongue lolling out, Milk Bone on my breath and green crumbs in my hair, I expected a pat on the head. I expected my mother to laugh or scratch behind my ears. Instead, she mouthed, "Get up." Instead, in a voice so low only a dog could hear it, she said, "I can't believe you're doing this to me."

"I can't believe you're doing this to me," she'd said when I told her I was pregnant.

"I can't believe you two are doing this to me," she says now after Aunt Thelma goes off down the hall whistling "Here Comes the Bride."

Dinner's almost ready. The sauce needs stirring.

My mother has always been proper. Her hair has always been perfect. Her shoes have always matched her purse.

"Never white after Labor Day," she says. "Patent leather is summer-only."

She's always worried about what's right and when.

She's always worried what people think, and how I, her only daughter, reflect on her.

Maybe it's because of the way she grew up, poor, during the Depression, her father keeping the house stocked with ice cream from money he made peddling bathtub gin.

Maybe it was because no one told her early on that she was beautiful and smart and good in the world.

Whatever the cause, insecurity and fear—of embarrassment, of losing control—have always been my mother's prime emotions.

"People talk," she says. "People say things."

I never knew why she cared so much.

"How could you?" my mother says now. "What will people think?"

This is when I swear off seeing her.

Chapter 51

I have eight ob-gyns. I have to pick one name to be designated my primary doctor, but the receptionist with the fingernails painted in red and white stripes like candy canes says there are no guarantees.

"We like you to get acquainted with all our doctors," she says, tapping one candied finger on my file. The file's still thin. By the time this is all over, it will be thick as a phone book. "You never know who's going to be on duty," she says and cracks the gum she's been chewing, "when it's time for you to pop."

Behind the receptionist's desk, there are pictures. Babies. Hundreds of them, push-pinned like insects to a giant corkboard. Over the corkboard, there's a sign that says "We Deliver."

On the counter in front of the reception window, there's a diapered-baby bobble-head and a huge jar of hard candy -- butterscotch rounds, caramels, Tootsie Rolls, desiccated peppermint circles that match the receptionist's nails. I'm queasy. I'm sweating. The receptionist doesn't notice. Or maybe she does and is just used to it.

She hands me a tiny plastic cup. "Tinkle sample," she says, and points to the bathroom.

Today I'm seeing Dr. Engle. Dr. Engle's mustache looks like a toupee. He has the bedside manner of a construction worker, and very small, very cold hands. I hope, whenever I do pop, Dr. Engle is on a golf course in another time zone.

During the pelvic exam, it's a challenge to tell what's a metal instrument and what's Dr. Engle. "A little pressure," he says, but everything's so cold, I'm almost numb.

After the exam, I sit up and notice paper. It's everywhere – the gown that ties in the front, the cover on the exam table, the privacy tent Dr. Engle drapes over my knees when he's peeking inside me like a coal miner and seeing me in a way I'll never see myself.

It's not just my sense of smell that's heightened. It's my awareness of sounds and textures. Everything is brighter, magnified -- the metal instruments on the metal tray, the zippered sound of the privacy curtain being pulled back. All this paper, crinkling like junk-food wrappers while Dr. Engle, quiet, a throat clearer, scribbles his notes, the pen scratching the paper like an itch.

I pull the paper gown tighter. I cross my arms and wish for a blanket. Dr. Engle looks at my chart. He spends a lot of time looking at my chart and very little time looking at me.

"You're gaining too fast," he says when he gets to my weight. He still doesn't look up, but he points his pen in my general direction and from the lines in his forehead I can see he's frowning. "May I ask what you're eating?"

By now I've discovered pregnancy manuals. This is how I know about heightened senses, what's normal, what's not. I've discovered *What to Expect When You're Expecting*, the royal guidebook of baby-making, which explains in detail what happens during each phase of pregnancy.

The book was a gift from Gina, whose sister has four kids. "My sister says you're going to need this," Gina said and at first I thought she was ridiculous. Then my stomach started to swell, my hips ached, my feet grew. There was sprouting and seeping and soon I had the book in bed with me and checked it like I was timing contractions.

Pregnancy symptoms are alphabetized in the back for easy reference. There's a pregnancy calendar that breaks down, month by month, what's happening to my body and my mind. There's something called The Best-Odds Diet, which the authors say offers the best chance for uber-baby results.

"I'm following the Best-Odds Diet," I tell Dr. Engle and

feel very smart. "Lots of fruit. Hard cheeses. No sushi. No lunch meat."

"What about juice?" Dr. Engle says. He looks at me now, peering over his little bifocals, making me feel transparent, like one of those plastic models of a woman, the kind schools use in anatomy classes, the kind with the removable breast plate, pop-out organs and detachable limbs.

I'm going through half a gallon of orange juice every day or two.

I figure this is a good thing.

"Lots of vitamin C," I say. "For the baby."

Dr. Engle says, "Lay off the juice."

Chapter 52

I lay off other things, too. *What to Expect* advises pregnant women take time for themselves. I should relax, it says. Avoid stress.

I've managed to avoid seeing my mother for two weeks. The guilt I feel is physical, like I've swallowed an alarm clock set to go off, but I'm angry, too, which helps.

She leaves messages. She needs prescriptions picked up from the pharmacy. She needs baking soda. I run the errands after school and leave everything on her porch. I run from the car to the porch and back, like a kid during Halloween, tick-tacking a house, ding-dong-ditching. I leave the car running, jump back in, hit the gas, and think about toilet-papering my own mother's shrubbery.

When her messages aren't about basic necessities, I try not to listen. The messages are carefully punctuated with sighs and wheezing and what may or may not be fake coughs.

"When I'm dead," she says, "you'll be sorry you didn't pick up this phone."

Chapter 53

According to the authors, *What to Expect When You're Expecting* is "not just an explanation of these nine amazing months; it's a celebration."

Things to celebrate: abdominal itchiness, bloodshot eyes, bloody show.

Leaky breasts, mucus changes, clumsiness.

Constipation, varicose veins, leg cramps.

Hemorrhoids, feet (increased size of), saliva (excessive), nipples (sore, cracked).

Flatulence, urinary incontinence, fecal incontinence.

The mask of pregnancy.

Hormonal shifts make some pregnant women's faces discolor. The discoloration is mostly around the eyes and cheeks, like a mask.

"Raccoon face," some women call it.

Chapter 54

I give in. The day's high is going to be somewhere in the 90s, with 100 percent humidity. My mother, who listens to weather reports like they are updates on the apocalypse, knows this.

"I'll try not to drop dead out there," she says on the answering machine.

"Don't fall for it," Dave says. He's half dressed – khakis, no shirt. He's rubbing his chest like he's trying to kick-start his circulation. He has to go in to work, even though it's Sunday, his day off, even though the store closes early and he'll be there for less time than it will take him to drive to the airport and back.

"This is non-negotiable," Elaine, his awful, mustached, Diet-Coke sucking, shoulder-pad wearing boss, says. But for once, I think Dave's relieved.

My mother, still on the answering machine, talks about gardening. Yard work. Late season tomatoes, some lingering squash. The tomato plants need to be re-staked. There are still peppers to think about.

"O.k. fine," she says. "Goodbye."

She says goodbye as if it's two words and each word is its own sentence. Even after she says it, she doesn't hang up. I can hear her on the line, breathing.

I pick up.

"Mom," I say, and she says, "Well, about time."

Chapter 55

When I get there, my mother's already outside, wrestling with a shrub. She has her electric clippers out. The clippers are cheap, flimsy, better for carving a ham than trimming trees. My mother is waving the clippers around and when she sees me pull up, she nearly lets them slip and comes close to slicing the electrical cord in half.

"You're going to electrocute yourself," I say as I get out of the car. "Be careful."

I wear an elasticized sundress and sneakers. My mother's decked out in her gardening gear – a lime green shorts set and running shoes, terry cloth sweatbands around her head and wrists. Her gray hair sprouts like a mushroom cloud over the top of the headband.

She looks like a bad-tempered tennis player, the kind who would give the finger to line judges at Wimbledon. When she's displeased, two lines, like an equals sign, are etched between her eyes. The lines are there now, finishing off their equation, sizing me up.

"Your ass," she says, pointing like I'm an orangutan at the zoo. "It's huge."

She says, "Are you even wearing a bra?"

Chapter 56

Some of it's about sex.

Even before I hit puberty, long before I became pregnant and puffed up like an overinflated pool toy, my mother started to fixate on my body, how it was changing into something dangerous.

"You don't want to send the wrong message," she'd say. "You don't want people to get ideas."

She'd watch me walk and shout, "Fries with that shake?" She bought me turtlenecks instead of the buttoned shirts I liked because buttoned shirts could easily be unbuttoned. And long before I needed a bra, in anticipation of the breasts to come, my mother made me wear Band-Aids, two of them on each nipple. "So they don't show through your clothes," she explained.

My flat chest, labeled with two flesh-colored Xs, looked obscene. It looked like a billboard for a porn movie.

"I don't see the big deal," I said to my mother then, I say to her now.

"I see it all right," my mother, an ironic double-D, said then, says now. "And if it weren't for me, everyone else would see it, too."

"I know one thing," she says. She grabs hold of my shoulders and spins me around once to take in the full horror. "If I'd ever been pregnant, I wouldn't have left the house for nine months. I wouldn't go anywhere looking like you."

Chapter 57

"I'm not the only woman who's found herself unexpectedly pregnant, you know," I say as my mother adjusts the straps on my sundress and stares at my chest, all that new-found cleavage. "It happens to a lot of people."

"If a lot of people jumped off the Westinghouse Bridge," my mother says, "would you jump too?"

She's been invoking this bridge my entire life. Two hundred and forty feet above the Turtle Creek Valley, the George Westinghouse Memorial Bridge spans the steel-and-concrete site of the former Westinghouse Electric Plant, in an area Pittsburghers call The Electric Valley.

The Westinghouse Bridge, built in 1932, is, as every native Pittsburgher knows, the bridge to take when things gets serious, which means it's the bridge to take when you're serious about killing yourself. A memorial pylon on the northwest corner of the bridge reads: "In Usefulness to Mankind."

"Useful like a heart attack," my mother says.

She stares at my chest and sighs.

"Who knows what people are saying about you," my mother says. "People talk, you know."

People do talk. They say things like "Take the bridge." They say, "Might as well jump." They say, "Nothing ever changes."

My mother tugs the elastic top of my sundress up to just underneath my shoulders, then steps back and sighs again.

"I hope you don't go out in public like that," she says.

She walks back to the garage, where she hands me a pair of gardening gloves, a bag of shredded pantyhose, and an armful of wooden stakes. The stakes are sharp and thick, good for killing vampires.

"Well," my mother says, "we might as well get to work."

Chapter 58

I throw ice cubes in the bathtub. I pummel pillows. I try deep breathing and pre-natal yoga.

"Yoga for preggos," Dave says.

Nothing works.

According to the pregnancy guidebooks, most pregnant women's mood swings and irritability subside after the first trimester. For me, it isn't true. I'm a funnel cloud of misery.

I pick fights. I pick them with Dave, over bills and dishes and the etiquette of drinking juice straight from the carton. I pick them with my mother, who I've taken to hanging up on mid-sentence. I pick them with Gina, who can't help that she's never been pregnant and can't relate.

When Gina suggests ear candling, a process in which she'd stick a hollowed out paper-and-beeswax candle in my ear, light it on fire and clear the toxins that are making me tweak, I tell her to go fuck herself.

"You're going to have to apologize for that one," she says, and I do, but now I think I hate Gina, my good and caring and best friend.

It might help if any one of my friends had ever been pregnant. They haven't, although Meg, my New York therapy friend, once walked around wearing a pregnancy pillow she stole from a maternity store dressing room. Meg and her boyfriend had broken up. She thought the best revenge would be for him to think she was pregnant.

"He has a mother complex," she explained. "This gets him both ways."

Meg read up on pregnancy and developed some symptoms, including a convincing pregnant waddle that, even when she gave up the pillow, was hard to shake.

But having a friend fake a pregnancy isn't the same as having a friend who has actually been pregnant. What I need now is insight, advice, a little empathy, but there isn't anyone – not June, not Gina, certainly not my mother, even though today she's the one I call because my belly button has started to pop.

Of all things I've been afraid of, this has been way up there. I've seen other pregnant women, tight t-shirts stretched over a nub you could hang a sweater on. The thought of my own belly button protruding from my body like a hitchhiking thumb is too much.

"Umbilicus," my mother, the nurse, says.

She prefers the proper names for everything. I never had colds growing up. I had upper respiratory infections. I did not have clubbed feet. I had a correctable deformity. I did not have a belly button or an innie. I had a concave umbilicus.

"There's a right way and a wrong way," my mother says.

She says, about my current umbilical distension, "Don't be ridiculous."

She says, "You're not the first woman who's ever been pregnant you know."

She says, "Stop thinking about yourself all the time."

She's right, but it's hard when my body keeps turning on me. It hasn't helped that none of the women I meet through work or doctors' visits or in grocery stores seem to be honest about pregnancy's downsides.

"I don't remember any pain," one woman, whose daughter was about a year old, said.

Another said, "I found the whole experience very soothing."

"I've never felt more peaceful," another one agreed.

"I never even had to wear maternity clothes," a tiny one with jelly bean feet and the posture of a dancer said. "I had a little bump out front, all baby. I hardly gained any weight at all."

The creepiest came from a woman in her late fifties who worked in public relations and knew how to put a spin on things.

"I had the best orgasm of my life during delivery," she said. "I'd get pregnant all over again just for that alone."

These women all seem to be smart, professional. But if I mention swelling, mood swings, or hormones, if I mention fears or doubts, they look at me as if my face has gone missing. They talk about pregnancy like it's a trip to the spa and, for one of them at least, a spa that offers happy endings.

I've never felt more alone.

"You and your feelings. You and your ideas," my mother says. "Stop thinking so much. Why can't you just be normal?"

Normal, to my mother, means a lot of things, but mostly it means doing things her way.

She's moved on from obsessing over the Vegas wedding to obsessing over baptisms and baby showers. She started crocheting heartbreakingly beautiful white baby blankets, and gave me two different sets of rosary beads, one pink, one blue.

"For the baptism," she says.

I haven't been to church in 15 years.

I don't want a baby shower. Baby showers are humiliating -- the pregnant woman in the center of the room, swollen and miserable, while normal-sized woman gape and giggle and play "Diaper Bag Bingo" and "Guess the Preggo's Waist Size."

The last shower I was at, we used pieces of yarn instead of a tape measure to guess. The pregnant woman's mother cut the yarn according to directions – one arm's length, two, more, less. Then each of us went up and wrapped our yarn around the pregnant woman's waist.

I've never been good at math or party games, and so I guessed long – about a whole arm's length too long -- and when I wrapped my yarn around her, the poor woman said, "Do I really look that big?" then broke into tears.

I tell my mother how I feel about showers and baptisms. She doesn't care.

"Can't you do anything right? Just one thing?" she says, and this time she hangs up first.

I lie down on the bed. Even though I'm not usually much of a crier, these days I can't help it. There's wadded-up tissue everywhere in the apartment. I find some not-too-crisp ones under my pillow and blow my nose loud and long because there's no one around to hear it.

<>

Dave works a lot at the bookstore. The more pregnant I become, the more hours Elaine makes him work. Elaine doesn't have a family. She doesn't have a husband or kids. It's either out of spite or callousness that she pretends Dave doesn't need to be home.

"It's urgent," she said when she called to tell him he'd have to spend four days in Atlanta at a bookstore managers convention.

"Is there someone else you could send?" he asked.

"I hope you're not trying to use your wife's pregnancy as an excuse," Elaine said.

And so Dave packed. Five plaid shirts, five pairs of plaid boxers, three pairs of khakis, a suitcase-sized box fan he'd use for white noise in the hotel room to help him sleep.

"She's an asshole," he said about Elaine. To me, he said, "Rest. Don't worry about anything. I'll call you."

That's where he is now. Atlanta.

I try not to run my hand over my belly, this alien thing, my body that's become not my body. Maybe those women I've met aren't lying. Maybe they're the type who are so happy to be pregnant, so amazed at the transformation, they take pictures of their bellies at all stages to chart their transition from ordinary human to something planetary. Maybe they take the pictures head on and from the side, like happy mug shots.

"The only things I've ever wanted were to be a wife and a mother," one of these women told me. "I never felt more fulfilled."

"Why can't you be normal?" my mother wants to know again and again. "Why can't you be satisfied?"

The stain on the ceiling over the bed is still there. It's growing, too, morphing from something that looked like Hitchcock into something more sprawling, bulbous, sinister. Pretty soon the ceiling might cave and water will gush down from whatever it is that's leaking up there and ruin everything. This makes me think about my water breaking, what that might be like. I hunt around with my fingers under the pillow, feeling for more tissue.

Chapter 59

In Atlanta, Dave's convention features pep rallies where all the managers have to dance to "Who Let the Dogs Out." They have to shout things in unison, things like "Shrink? Not on my shift!"

"What's shrink?" I ask Dave when he calls.

"Their dicks," he says. "Profits. Either. Both."

He sounds exhausted. He sounds sad. He calls from his hotel room. In the background, I hear the fan whirring. The fan and the long distance connection hollow everything out.

As the highlight of the convention, the company president, a tiny shoebox of a man, rides in on a horse, just like John Wayne or Napoleon. He rides the horse through the hotel lobby, across Turkish carpets and glistening chandeliers, and straight into the hotel's grand ballroom, where he introduces a Conway Twitty cover band and makes every one of the managers stick around to listen. A company employee, a manager like Dave, is ordered to follow behind the horse with a dustpan and broom, ready to scoop horse shit. During another dinner, the president threatens to fire everyone.

"I'm losing my mind," Dave says, and I say, "What about me?"

"People live through pregnancy all the time," he says.

I say, "Lots of people have jobs they hate."

It's nearly 700 miles from Pittsburgh to Atlanta.

The distance between my husband and me is more than that.

Chapter 60

When we fight, we throw things – the phone, books, dinner plates, wine glasses. This time, I throw one of Dave's shoes. I'm going for his head, but I'm not even close.

The shoe hits the wall and takes a chip out of the landlord's plaster. It's a heavy shoe, a thick-soled Dr. Marten. When it hits the wall, it sounds thick and fleshy, like what leather was once, a body.

Dave bends down and picks it up.

"Nice," he says.

He says, "Now give me the other one."

I'm on the bed, feeling hugely pregnant, propped on a mound of pillows wedged into a C-shape against the headboard. I can fight sitting down. I can fight just about anywhere, all the time. I love to fight.

I stuff the other shoe under a blanket.

"No," I say.

"Give it," Dave says again. He holds out his hand.

"Fuck you," I say.

"Give me the goddamned shoe," he says.

Inside me, our son kicks so hard it feels like my ribs will snap.

"I'm sick of doing this alone," I say.

"Quit acting like a mill wife," Dave says.

"I'm fucking sick of it," I say, and he lunges for the other shoe. Even propped up, I'm fast. I hurl the other shoe across the room.

"Fetch," I say.

He says, "Fucking mill wife," and I say, "Good dog."

Maybe I want to see if he'll hit me. Maybe I want to push us both to a place where we can never come back. The look on Dave's face is a lightning storm, but when he walks across the room, bends down to pick up the shoe, when he sits down on the floor and puts on one shoe then the other, when he gets up to leave, he's calm, which is, maybe, worse.

He says. "I'll be back for the rest of my things in a few days."

"Coward," I say, and then he says what neither of us has said through all these months.

"You wanted this baby," he says. "It was your choice. No one forced you. You know I have a job. You know we need money. You know I can't leave my job where I make the money we need to go with you to every doctor visit. Going to the doctor with you would be better than going to work, and you're awful so that says something about how I feel about my job. Now don't talk to me anymore."

And I say, "Yeah, fuck you."

"You wanted this baby," he says. "You fucking bitch. Start acting like it."

"You're the bitch," I say.

"I'm the guy with the job he hates, who gets yelled at every day by a 300-pound woman who hates me because I'm going to be a father," he says. "I'll be standing in a bookstore, which should be my dream job, and I'll be loving books and my fat fucking boss will hate me for that too. So why don't you call off from your cushy teaching job where everyone thinks it's great you're having a baby. And no offense, asshole, I have ten times the publications you do, I'm ten times more qualified, and before you respond, fuck you."

Chapter 61

Dave comes back hours later. I'm not sure where he's been or where he planned to go.

He comes back and sits down on a corner of the bed. The bed is covered with tissues, balled up, shredded. He has to clear a space to sit.

I don't move.

Up from the street, there are sirens, a bass pulse from the bar next door. The bar's called The Smiling Moose. Before that, it was called Delfonzo's. Before that, Lucky's,

No matter what the owners change the name to, there are always fights. It's one of those places where people can't get along. I don't know why. There's a fight there now. I can hear yelling, but I can't make out the words. It could be about the jukebox. It could be about a girl. It could be about nothing or everything. There's the sound of breaking glass.

It's the weekend. Everyone is in the clubs and bars, trying to hook up, fall in love, drink or fuck their way out.

There are cops out on weekends. The lights from all the police cars match the blue and red neon on the sign for a jazz club two blocks down called The Blue Note.

On Sundays, Chizmo Charles plays there. Chizmo's an old Pittsburgh blues man. He wears a brown leisure suit with white stitching around the pockets. He wears gold rings and gold chains. He's missing some teeth, but his shoes are as shined as his voice is graveled. He sings about love and loss and ending up in heaven sitting down.

Dave and I used to go see him when we first got together, before I was pregnant, before Dave got a job he hates.

"This should be our Sundays," Dave said back then, meaning instead of church we'd do the blues with Chizmo and his beautiful groupies, old barflies with faded butterfly tattoos who pound the bar and sing along.

"Hope is hard to come by and you ladies sure give a poor man hope," Chizmo always says to them.

I haven't thought of Chizmo for a while, the way he'll sing right to the loneliest looking women at the bar. He'll lean in and touch their faces and pass them the mic. He'll pace, a preacher testifying, while his bass player keeps rhythm underneath like a pulse.

The women, even the most broken-looking ones, love this. They smile and flirt and lift their blouses and flash Chizmo, nearly 90 with a face like a relief map, their bras.

What moves people to do what we do, I don't know.

I think it's almost always about the heart, about regret and longing, those two sad oyster-faced twins.

"What's happening to us?" I say to Dave when I'm done crying.

He says, "I don't know."

He lies down, fully dressed, his shoes still on.

Chapter 62

My mother wants to be in the delivery room. I don't want her there. We're in the car driving from her heart doctor's office after a check-up. She's doing well, so he's adjusted her medications.

"You'll be less tired," he said. "You should have more energy."

She already does. Today she wants to stop by K-Mart to buy some baby gear – onesies, crib sheets. "Don't wait until the last minute like you always do," she says.

Then she wants to hit two grocery stores. She has the grocery flyers in the backseat.

"How about just one," I say, "Pick one," and she says, "Giant Eagle has chicken on sale. Shop n' Save has ground meat, buy one get one." She says, "I'm not like you." She says, "I know money doesn't grow on trees."

I barely fit behind the steering wheel. I can barely reach the brake. I'm wearing Dave's shoes because my feet are too swollen for anything else. I'm so tired I feel like I'm walking through a swamp.

"You can't lie around in bed all day," my mother says. "I'm a nurse. I know. You have to get up. You have to move." She grabs hold of my arms and pulls them back and forth like ski poles.

I don't want to move. I want to lie down and sleep this off. I want this to be over.

The contractions have started, the practice ones, Braxton-Hicks. I'm getting scared because I think I won't know the real contractions when they come. I'm afraid when I do realize, it will be too late and my water will break and flood the produce aisle and I'll have the baby right there, next to the lettuce, on the cold tile floor at Giant Eagle, where the chicken really is a bargain at $1.50 off a pound.

I check *What to Expect* over and over. I read a section on contractions, labor and delivery, then I forget what I've read and have to read it again.

Short-term memory loss, forgetfulness, trouble concentrating. These are all symptoms of the third trimester.

So is fear.

"Don't worry," Dr. Engle said this week as he puttered under the paper tent he'd built over my knees, measuring my cervix, checking for softening, checking for signs. "Usually with the first one, labor's long. Those people who give birth in cabs, those are usually second and third pregnancies. Sometimes those babies just drop right out. You'll have lots of time."

He patted my knee like a coach and went on rooting.

Between my own belly and the tent, I could barely see the top of his head, the little light that perched there, right in the middle of his forehead. It felt like his whole arm was inside me, trying to turn me inside out, and maybe it was.

Long labor, he said, like it was something to look forward to.

Dave and I had bailed on the recommended Lamaze classes after just one session. Had we stuck them out, maybe I'd be less nervous. Maybe I'd feel more in control. But the woman who'd been running the class looked like a nun. She had very short hair and thick glasses and wore a long flowery Laura-Ashley type dress with a little lace collar. The first half of the first session – which is as far as Dave and I made it before we snuck out a back door, down a fire escape, and across the parking lot for double cheeseburgers and fries – was spent on diapers.

"Aren't these just the cutest things," the woman said. She held up two different diapers. Both diapers were fancy, expensive-looking, with pink or blue patterns on the butts.

"But now, she says, "watch this."

The woman poured a glass of water, first on one diaper, then the other. She waited a moment, then held them up. There were giant smiley faces on both diapers. These hadn't been there before.

"These diapers let you know when they're wet!" she said, squealing like she'd just won something on a game show. "Isn't that amazing?"

Other parents in the room nodded and said, "ooh" and "ah," like the woman had just set off fireworks. Some took notes.

"Things like this take some of the guesswork out of parenting," the woman said. She made the diapers do a little dance across the table before she set them down and said, "Any questions?"

"Do you think we're locked in?" I whispered to Dave, and he whispered back, "Let's get the hell out of here."

And so we'd had nothing else – no coach-training, no instruction in meditative pain-reducing techniques, no exercises in deep breathing, no knowing when and when not to push.

"I do yoga," I said to Gina. "I think I can control my breathing."

I said, "Who needs Lamaze."

I said, "I'm getting an epidural. Maybe two."

I said, "Doesn't the doctor tell you when to push?"

Gina said, "I don't know," and neither did I.

Now I can't sleep. I'm always uncomfortable and the baby kicks whenever I try to rest. I have nightmares – the expected kind, full of blood and screams and giving birth to something not quite human. But there is something else, too. My mother's going on about it now.

"I want to be there," she's saying.

"You can't," I say. "Your heart. It's too much stress."

"I think I know what kind of stress I can handle," she says and slaps the sun visor down.

"I'd worry," I say.

"I'm a nurse," she says.

"You haven't been a nurse in years," I say, "and this is different."

"How?" she says, and slaps the visor up, then down again, like a face. "How is it different?"

"I'm your daughter," I say, and she says, "Like that matters."

Growing up, I'd been in the hospital so much. The surgeries for my legs and feet, those correctable deformities, began before my parents adopted me and went on until I was nine or 10. I'd often be in the hospital where my mother worked. This was Braddock Hospital, just outside of Pittsburgh. My mother would work it out with the doctors and the other nurses. She'd get transferred to my floor. She'd sleep overnight next to me on a cot. The nurses would bring me treats, extra blankets, comic books.

One time, an off-duty nurse came in with a huge box of jeans for me to choose from, all of them with embroidery on the pockets, rhinestone hearts and flowers, very fancy. I could choose whichever pair I liked. I could take my time looking. She held up one pair, then another, then another. "For when you get out of those casts," she'd said, and I felt like a celebrity. All of this was because I was my mother's daughter, Bertie Jakiela's girl.

At work, they called my mother by her last name. Some people called her Sarge. "I run a tight ship," my mother would say, but most of her co-workers seemed to like her.

When I wasn't in the hospital, when I was at home and things were fine, my mother worked only on the weekends. I'd sit on her bed while she dressed for work – white pantyhose, the white dress uniform she'd tailor to her curves, sturdy square-tipped shoes that she'd keep white with polish.

Her hair was very black. The nurse's cap set it off. She pinned the cap to her hair with white bobbie pins. When I'd get older, she'd ask me to help pin the back. She did her make-up, carefully – fake eyelashes, pink lipstick.

"It's good to look nice. It cheers people up," she said, and she did look nice. She looked beautiful. Dressed up like this, my mother was transformed. She was happy. She was herself. "This is all I ever wanted," she says about her years in nursing school, about how hard it was, about what it meant to her to graduate.

My mother was a wonderful nurse. I can't imagine how hard it was for her to care for me all those years, my legs in casts up to my hips. I can't imagine what it was like for her to watch me go through surgery after surgery, each time having to go over the risks, each time knowing too much about the possibilities. But she did, and she was good and steady. As far back as I can remember, each time, before I went into surgery, she'd say the same thing. "Heart of my heart," one of the clichés she gathered up like angel pins, of course, but what she meant was that even though I wasn't hers by birth, I was and always would be hers.

My mother's face was always the first one I'd see when I woke up in the recovery room.

"We were always so close," my mother would say about our relationship. "Until she became a teenager. Until she went to college. Then all hell broke loose."

Until I wanted a life separate from my mother's.

Until I wanted something all my own.

This baby, this birth, this moment.

Having my mother in the delivery room would be, based on the way she's been acting, disastrous. I don't want that, and I feel selfish not wanting it, but my own selfishness has to outdo my mother's selfishness or else she'll own my life, my child, everything.

"Your heart," I say.

"Quit with your excuses," she says.

I say, "And besides, how would we get you there?"

"Dave," she says, "Dave will come and get me."

"I'll be in labor," I say.

"So?" she says.

"Don't you think he should be there?" I say, and she says, with years of medical knowledge to back her up, "It's your first one. There will be time."

Chapter 63

Women who take childbirth classes, according to *What to Expect*, have shorter labors. Women who take childbirth classes have fewer complications. Women who take childbirth classes are less likely to panic.

I'm home in bed when my water breaks. At least I think my water breaks. It's nothing like what I expected, no gushing, just a slow trickle, like a leaky water balloon. At first I think I've peed myself, and then I realize probably not.

Dave's in the shower, getting ready for work. I yell but he can't hear me over the water. I yell again and try not to panic. The contractions are there, a large fist opening and closing inside me. They're no worse than bad cramps and I think, o.k., breathe. I roll off the bed and start getting dressed. I already have a bag packed with new pajamas and a robe, some onesies, receiving blankets and a welcome-home outfit for our son, who we are naming Locklin after our friend Gerald Locklin, a great poet and good man.

June is going with us to the hospital. June, not my mother, will be in the delivery room. June is calm, centered, a former hippie and the only person other than Dave who I could imagine watching me go through what *What to Expect* calls the "miracle of birth." All that blood and piss. All the possible threats and screaming.

June's been there for the births of her two nephews. She's calmly walked through all of this before and comes with an excellent reference from her sister-in-law, who now says of June's mid-wife abilities -- "If it weren't for her, I would have stabbed someone."

I love June. She'll be good company for Dave. She'll keep things calm.

"You have got to be kidding me," my mother said when I told her.

"We'll call you as soon as he's out," I said. "Dave will come and get you and bring you straight to the hospital."

"I can't believe you're doing this to me," she said.

"It's not about you this time," I said, and tried not to feel guilty about it.

When Dave gets out of the shower, I point to the suitcase I've left near the door and say, "I think my water broke," and he says, "What do you mean think?" and I say, "I'm pretty sure," and he says, "Sure, sure, or pretty sure?"

I know even now he's dreading calling Elaine to tell her he won't be able to make it in to work and that there's a good chance she'll tell him to drop me off at the hospital and come in anyway.

There's a list on the fridge, steps I'm supposed to take, and I take them. I'm dressed. Packed. I call the ob-gyn office.

"I think my water broke. I'm having contractions," I say. It's Nancy on the phone. Nancy's the nurse I see every visit. She's the one who tells me to close my eyes when she weighs me so I won't see the numbers going up. She's the one who takes my blood pressure, asks if I'm following the doctors' advice to lay off the juice, and shows me pictures of her children and grandchildren.

When Dr. Engle and the other assembly-line doctors make pregnancy feel like an anatomy class, Nancy, in her teddy-bear covered smocks, her gray hair permed into a little cloud, makes it feel human again, like something we're going through together.

"O.k. honey, stay calm," Nancy says. "How far apart are the contractions?"

"O.k. honey," Nancy says. "The hospital knows you're coming. Good luck."

Before we leave, Dave calls Elaine. She says, "Great. That's just great." She says, "You'll be in tomorrow, right? This is not an excuse."

Chapter 64

I'm in labor for 23 hours. Three hours of that are pushing. I end up with a face-full of broken blood vessels and an emergency c-section.

This isn't, I'll learn later, that unusual.

If every woman I talked to before I gave birth told me the Disney version of pregnancy and labor, every woman I'll talk with afterwards will offer up a horror story.

"Fifteen hours," Jennifer will say. "I was in labor fifteen hours before they gave me drugs. The nurse kept telling me to keep it down, that my screaming was scaring other patients."

"They put my epidural in wrong," Cathy will say. "They let a med student do it. For practice. I could feel everything, but only on one side. It felt like I was being pulled apart by two trucks. Nothing prepares you for that. Nothing."

"I wanted to kill him," Trish will say.

Her husband, a music critic with strong opinions about nearly everything, just shrugs. "See," she'll say. "That's what he was doing the whole time in the delivery room, like he was helpless. The nurse had to hold me down at one point to keep me from getting to him."

Maybe all those women I met during my pregnancy, the ones with all the happy stories, were just trying to be kind.

Or maybe they really didn't remember. Memory in the best times can be slippery. What I remember from labor and delivery are random moments, snapshots that come in and out of focus, out of order, out of time.

My water hasn't broken all the way. A nurse in a pink smock bends down, does something I can't feel, then jumps back. There's the sound of water pouring on the floor, though I can't see. I'm embarrassed. "I'm sorry," I say, and she says, "Don't worry. You missed me."

<>

A nurse gives me Pitocin. She says, "I'm sorry but you will feel this."

<>

The contractions come, one after the other, trains being pulled hard uphill, then the held breath, then the collapse back down.

<>

June and Dave are hungry and talking about pizza. There's a place down the street that delivers. They're trying decide what to get. They settle on sausage and pepperoni, spinach on half. I lean over the bed and throw up on the floor.

<>

I'm hunched over a pillow and someone I don't know, a doctor, an intern, puts the epidural in. I love her very much.

Dave feeds me ice chips. His face is close to mine. He looks worried. He smells like pizza.

<>

A nurse, who looks very tired, tells me to push. "You can do this," she says, though I can tell from her voice she knows I can't.

<>

In another room, a woman screams. I do not believe this woman is me.

<>

June says, "His head's right there. I see it."

<>

The doctor, one of the only ones I haven't met at the ob-gyn office, says, "I think he really likes it in there."

<>

In the operating room, I'm relieved to be strapped down. A new nurse is there. She's on my left. Dave's on my right. Both sets of eyes, hers and his, are blue above blue surgical masks. The nurse puts on glasses. She looks, probably because of the drugs, because all of the blue, like a fish.

<>

The fish nurse gives me morphine. She says, "This is the good stuff."

<>

There's a sound like a band saw. Dave looks like he might pass out. The nurse sends him into the other room to breathe. He's gone a while. He comes back, shuffling in blue booties, a tiny puddle of sweat pooled in his ear.

<>

From the other side of the blue tent strung up between me and the doctor, there's crying. It's loud. The fish nurse says, "'Listen to the lungs on that one."

<>

When they bring Locklin around to show him to us, he's still crying. Dave is crying. I think I'm crying, too. My arms are strapped down. I can't touch anyone or wipe my face. The fish nurse takes a tissue and wipes it for me.

<>

Two nurses wheel me out, back to the delivery room where I'd been. Another nurse brings Locklin in. She lays him on my belly and he scuttles up like a crab and latches on to my right breast. "He's very smart," the nurse says.

<>

It will take years before my son looks the way he did in my dreams, but the hands were there from the start. In pictures, he looks like he has two starfish on the ends of his arms.

<>

Locklin suckles and pulls, ravenous. A bird trying to open an oyster.

My son's eyes are closed. The skin on his back is wrinkled. His fingers are splayed on my breast. He looks like an angry salamander, tiny old man, most beautiful thing.

Chapter 65

The nurses take us to a room, where we all pass out. Locklin, Dave, June and me. I wake up and hear everyone snoring, Locklin included.

A woman comes into the room. She looks familiar. Maybe she's the same woman from the childbirth classes. I don't know. She's perky, loud. She carries a small bathtub.

"I'm here to teach you how to bath your baby," she says.

"You're kidding," I say, and feel my eyes closing.

Dave wakes up, too. He says, "She's been in labor for a day. She's just out of surgery."

The woman cocks the tub on one hip. She says, to Dave, to me, "I'm on a schedule. It's now or never. Do you want to learn or not?"

Chapter 66

Someone grabs my arm, then pulls, hard.

It could be anyone – the baby-bath trainer, the perky phlebotomist built like a test tube who keeps sticking me in my sleep, the little old ladies of La Leche League who stop by in shifts to see if I've mastered the football hold and if my son has mastered proper breastfeeding techniques.

"I need to see him latch on," the last La Leche woman said when she stopped by earlier.

"He latched on right after he was born," Dave said.

"You don't know that," the woman said and jotted a note on her clipboard. "We have to check for a good seal."

"Like Tupperware?" Dave said, and the La Leche woman didn't smile. Dave didn't smile, either. His clothes were rumpled. He was exhausted and had to leave soon to pick up my mother. Later, he had to go to work.

"I need you here," Elaine said. "I need to be here, too," Dave said, and Elaine said, "That's your problem, isn't it?"

"I'm sleeping most of the time anyway," I say to make Dave's having to go to work better than it is. "I'll be fine."

It's not really sleep. It's more like a drugged haze that gets cracked open by nurses and doctors and my son's wailing as they wheel him down the hall for feedings. "This one sure lets you know what he wants when he wants it," one nurse says as she hands him over. "This one's not going to let anybody forget about him."

The nurse's skin is so white it melts into her uniform. She looks exhausted and not very fond of my son. Already, I feel like a bad mother. Maybe I should keep him in the room with me and not send him to the nursery. Maybe he cries the whole time. Maybe he's pushing things.

I remember an old joke – nurses losing patients – and a story I've heard about a nurse who was fired because she taped pacifiers to babies' mouths. When asked if she worried the babies might suffocate, she said, "They wouldn't stop crying and I needed some peace."

Everyone here could use some peace, or at least some sleep.

Whoever it was the first time pulls again, harder.

Then it's more like a slap.

"We're o.k.," I say, without opening my eyes. I try to move my arm, but it's heavy with tubes and wires. "Thanks for checking."

"Thanks for nothing," the voice says. "Get up." And I know, even through the veil of morphine, it's my mother, Sarge, the former nurse.

"Everybody straightened up when they saw her coming," my mother's friend and co-worker Marcia always said. "Even the tough patients wouldn't mess with her because they knew she'd raise holy hell."

The stories Marcia told about my mother had become mythological. My mother with a fake hypodermic the size of a salami. My mother who, when a patient threw a loaded bedpan at her, filled it with water and threw it back. I don't know if she ever really brandished an enema bottle like a gun or slipped rude doctors brownies laced with laxatives or whether, when confronted with a senile patient proud of his newfound hard-on, my mother threw a hospital gown over his lap, handed him a pill cup and said, "That's nothing to get worked up over. I've seen better pup tents."

One thing, though, is certain. My mother had been denied her delivery-room rights. She is angry. Now she is here in what she'd call "a professional capacity."

Before I can move or speak, she pulls off my blankets. She's down at my legs now, trying to jerk them off the bed. Dave tries to grab her hands. She swats him off and gets hold of an ankle. I pull my leg back and feel dizzy. The pain in my incision is sharp and fast. Dave says, "That's enough." He says, "Stop it."

My mother tosses the blanket on the floor. It lands at the entrance to the bathroom where later I'll pass out, slipping and falling on my own blood after another nurse who is not my mother will succeed in getting me out of bed. The nurse will leave me alone in the bathroom, where I'll find myself on the floor and have to crawl to reach the call button. Two nurses will have to lift me and carry me back to bed. There will be more blood.

None of this will be negligent or cruel. It's standard practice. It's probably what my mother is trying to do now, but it seems violent and too much.

"You," she's saying. The finger she points is so worked up it shakes, and even drugged I think about her heart. "You need to get up. You need to walk around.
And you," she points at Dave, "need to stop babying her."

While I'd been dozing and fending off La Leches, Dave had done what he'd promised. He'd driven to Trafford, picked up my mother and brought her to the hospital to meet her grandson.

She'd dressed beautifully – in a purple velvet pantsuit and the purple starburst-petal choker. She'd done her hair. She'd put on lipstick. She'd dressed for a happy occasion, which it should have been, but from the moment she walked into the hospital room, everything turned. And maybe because I'm drugged and tired, at first I don't know what's happening or why.

On the drive over, they hit traffic, construction. It took a long time. The drive hadn't been pleasant. The drive back would be worse. On the way over, Dave tried to fill my mother in – the details, complications. He told her about all the hours in labor, the pushing, how nothing worked, the emergency surgery. "We're all pretty wrecked," he said. "It was that awful."

My mother wasn't moved. She felt she was strong enough to have been there, healthy enough to handle things. I'd denied her a moment she was entitled to, a moment neither of us could ever get back. It is something neither she nor I will forget. My reasons don't matter. Here, in this hospital room, my mother plans to show me she is neither weak nor someone who will tolerate being shut out.

"I know one thing," she says. "This wouldn't have happened if I'd been here. These doctors wouldn't have pussyfooted around, not if I had been here."

"You people," she says, "have no idea what you're dealing with."

She pushes the button that raises and lowers my bed.

She goes for my legs. I pull a pillow over my stomach and try to sit up. She almost knocks over the IV to get at me. She doesn't seem to notice. I'm sure we're making a huge fuss, but none of the nurses come to see what's happening. My bed whirs up and down. My mother is swatting. Dave keeps trying to get between us. He takes a few hits before he says, "We need to go now. I'm serious. It's time to leave."

Later, my mother will tell the story this way: "I walked into that room and I was so shocked. Shocked! I didn't even recognize my own daughter, my poor little girl. She looked like she'd been beaten. I wouldn't have let that happen. I wouldn't have let them do that to her." She'll be all sweetness and light, an angel on a stick pin.

But now, with Dave holding her back, she says, "What are you going to do? Lie there like a lump? Jesus Mary and Joseph, get up."

I pull the pillow tighter across my stomach. "I'm tired, mom," I say. "I'm sore. I'm in pain. The baby cries constantly."

Her laugh sounds bitter and edged, like it could cut. "You don't know pain," she says. "I've had open heart surgery. That's pain. This is nothing. Now get up."

I close my eyes and don't move. I wish her gone.

Dave leads her out of the room by her elbow.

"She can just lie there for all I care," my mother says. "She can clot up. She can lie there and rot in her own stink for all I care since she knows so much."

I don't even know if my mother has seen her grandson.

I don't even know if she knows his name.

Chapter 67

Dave and my mother are gone. A nurse wheels Locklin back into the room. He is, as usual, wailing. His fists are red. His feet are red. They poke and thrash above the plastic bassinette, like he is kicking and sucker-punching the whole world.

The nurse lifts him, then puts him down, still writhing, on a blanket she's laid out on the bed.

"If you want, I'll show you how to swaddle him," she says. "They like it. It makes them feel secure."

The blanket she uses has tiny mittens and sleds all over it. It's January. A new year. The blanket is flannel, all soft and worn, and I wonder how many babies before my son have found comfort there.

The nurse folds the blanket into a triangle. With one hand, she holds onto Locklin, his legs and arms flailing like angry drunks. With the other hand, she maneuvers the points of the blanket. It seems intricate, like origami. Within seconds, Locklin's contained. His crazed little face peeps out from a tight cocoon. He cries, but calmer. The nurse hands him to me like a package from a deli.

"You can unwrap him if you'd like, but I thought you'd want to know how to do it," she says.

I must look confused or amazed. I must look how I feel, like nothing will ever make sense again.

"Don't worry," she says. "This all looks more complicated than it is."

Chapter 68

My mother to Dave on the car ride home:

"You think you can get by on love and kisses, you have another thing coming.

"Now you're in for it.

"Now you'll see what everything's about."

Chapter 69

It's snowing. Dave is in work clothes. He tries to get the car seat in place. Neither of us had thought about doing this sooner.

The car is parked in front of the hospital lobby, where I'm signing the discharge papers and a nurse is waiting to wheel Locklin and me out to the car in a wheelchair. All around us, pregnant women are coming in, families with new babies are going out. The hospital is busy as an airport. Everything moves except for us.

The player piano in the lobby, a beautiful glossy baby grand, plinks out jazz. Car hops park and retrieve cars. Happy parents and grandparents pose for pictures with newborns wrapped up in fuzzy snow suits. The phone at the switchboard doesn't stop. The nurse looks at her watch.

"Do you think he needs help?" she says. She points outside, where Dave bangs his head on the car door. "Do you think he knows what he's doing?"

"Sure," I say. "We'll be o.k."

Once Dave gets the car seat in, he buckles Locklin down. Locklin hates it. He punches and kicks the whole way home. I reach back to make sure he doesn't cry so hard his head flops down. Dave looks like he might pull over and stop the car. He tried to get the day off and once again Elaine wouldn't have it.

"How long are you going to keep this up?" she wants to know.

It's minutes from the hospital to the apartment, but it feels longer. Dave and I don't talk. It's hard to hear or concentrate over the sound of Locklin wailing. In the hospital it was bad enough, but here, in an enclosed space, his cries could rip steel.

When we get to our block, there's nowhere to park. Dave does a few loops, drops his hands on the steering wheel, more defeated than angry, then settles for an illegal spot four blocks away.

"Let the cops come and fucking tow it," he says as he struggles to pop Locklin out, car seat and all.

Dave carries Locklin like a picnic basket. I wish for the wheelchair. I waddle behind and hold my stomach and am careful not to trip. We go past the tattoo shop where I fell down and the old man stepped over me. "We've all been there," he said and I think, no, we haven't.

We go past Dee's Bar, a new Starbucks and a massage parlor. The massage parlor's called Elite Spa. When it first opened, I was happy. I thought it was a real spa. Then they covered the windows with dark gray curtains and I noticed all the employees seemed to be women dressed in fetish wear. In the mornings, when the spa opened, it wasn't unusual to see a nurse and a dominatrix, a business woman and a schoolgirl in knee socks, all going inside.

"It's like living next door to a punch line," I say whenever the subject of Elite comes up. But this is our neighborhood. This is where we take our son.

"You will come and stay with me," my mother said. She called the hospital after the scene in the room. She never apologized, but she kept calling.

"I'll be fine," I said. "Besides, Dave has to work. He couldn't commute from your house. It would take hours."

"He can stay there," she said. "You and the baby will come here. He can visit."

Move my son a few doors down from a massage parlor or move him away from his father? A dominatrix or my mother?

Every step feels like the next one will rip me open. I lag behind and Dave goes on ahead, Locklin in his carseat sledgehammering against his thigh. I can hear Locklin crying, his voice carried back on a cloud of bus exhaust.

At least two of us here hate our lives.

Chapter 70

We climb the four flights up to the apartment to find it's flooded. The icemaker blew up. There is a brown pond around the refrigerator and what looks like a burn mark on the wall. Water is everywhere. In the bedroom, the brown carpet looks swampy and smells worse.

Dave's parents have already arrived. They've done their best to make a proper homecoming. Locklin's bassinet is set up in the bedroom. There are balloons and streamers. My mother-in-law Jan has posted a Welcome Home Mommy & Locklin sign she made on her computer back in Michigan. She brought a cake. She brought ice cream.

"Calcium," she says, smiling. "You can eat as much as you want and no one can say anything about it."

My father-in-law Charlie is on his knees, pointing a flashlight under the refrigerator. Both Jan and Charlie are smiling, like everything's perfect, like everything's fine. I'm so grateful they pretend not to see things, that they don't let on that they know the truth about our lives.

"Those stairs must have been awful to climb," Jan says. Her hair is perfect, her nails manicured, her clothes wrinkle-free even after five hours in a car. She hugs and nudges me past the mound of sludge she's swept up from around the refrigerator. "Why don't you lie down? Why don't you get some rest?"

Charlie clicks off the flashlight. "Well I'm sure your landlord will come right over and fix this," he says. "Let's give her a call."

Jan fluffs some pillows on the bed and points me to them. "Your downstairs neighbor," she says. "What's his name? The one with the interesting music. He seems nice." She says, "I think this might be leaking in his apartment."

Through all this, Locklin's been crying. He started as soon as Dave got him through the doorway. I sit down on the bed and Dave unbuckles the car seat and hands Locklin to me. I don't take off my coat. I tuck Locklin underneath, turn toward the wall, and let him feed. Feeding, it seems, is the only thing that keeps him quiet for long.

"Don't start that," the La Leche women warned. "Don't you let him graze on you."

"We'll just leave you two alone," Jan says, smiling, but there's nowhere, really, for any of us to go. She tries to close the door between the bedroom and kitchen, but it's thin as balsa wood. It's wet and bent like cardboard. I'm not sure when the ice maker first broke, but the bottom of the door looks like it's already starting to mold.

Underneath my coat, Locklin sucks hard. He pounds his fist against my breast like it's a jukebox. He curls his nugget feet into my ribs, just the way he did when he was inside of me. I rock as much as I can without the incision aching. I make soothing, clucking sounds until they catch in my throat.

Chapter 71

Jan brings Locklin to me for his feedings that first night. I stay in bed. She brings me tea and changes Locklin's diapers. Charlie gets the pond in the kitchen under control and handles my landlord the next morning.

And then they go back to Michigan.

I want them to stay. Maybe they want to stay but are afraid to overstep. For all they know, I've had a baby in six months. I don't know how they're dealing with that because no one brings it up.

Gina's out of town for work. Dave's at the bookstore. My mother is my mother. I'm alone here with my son, who won't stop crying. I rock and pace and sing. I let him graze. When Dave gets home, we take him for rides in the car and do loops around a Taco Bell parking lot. This calms him so he'll fall asleep in the car for a few minutes. When he wakes up again, he's furious, like he's been duped.

I give him baths. Baths are supposed to be soothing. I use his baby bathtub, and then, when he seems to hate that, I try the sink, which works a bit better. He seems to like closed spaces. He likes to be held. I remember the nurse who taught me how to swaddle him.

"It makes them feel secure," she said.

"He's colicky, that's what," my mother says when I call. "Try Mylicon."

She says, "If you weren't so stubborn, you could bring him here. I could take care of this."

I try to wait until Dave goes to work before I join in and start crying myself. This is how my son and I spend our day, weeping and holding each other.

When Dave comes home, I try to pretend things are better. "Really, when you're gone, sometimes he's happy," I say over our son's screaming. "This is just his tired time."

Chapter 72

Locklin is a little over a month old when the crying gets worse. George pounds on the ceiling downstairs with a broom. He threatens to tell the landlord and have us evicted.

"Look," George said once when he came upstairs. "You have to get him to chill. This really isn't a good place for a baby." He means the walls are too thin, the floors. He means he can hear everything.

George is right. I am a horrible mother to bring my son here and expect him not to cry.

Downstairs George turns his whale-song music up. When that doesn't work, he pounds, which makes Locklin cry even more.

When nothing I can do will soothe my son, when he won't nurse, I call the doctor's office.

"Date of birth?" the nurse on call says, her voice flatlined. "And he's been here before?"

These, I will learn, are the same two questions they'll ask for years.

"Some babies are just sensitive," she says when I tell her what's happening. "Have you tried Mylicon?"

I expect the nurse to do something. I expect her to care. I don't yet know I'm one of dozens who'll call today. I don't yet know that pediatricians' offices have unspoken rules. I don't yet know that as a parent, there are certain words I'm supposed to use, that I will sometimes have to demand that my child be seen.

"They said some babies are just like this," I tell Gina. She's here with me and Locklin. She pretends the crying doesn't bother her. She has two days off from the road, then she has to go back to Ohio. She's doing consulting work. Her company keeps her in a hotel room with rust-colored water and bugs. "I can't do this much longer," she says. I've never heard her give up on anything before.

Gina bends over Locklin and tries to tickle his feet. He kicks. She picks him up and tucks his head between her neck and shoulder. He thrashes and one of his fists get stuck in her hair. Gina works it loose, then brings him down and cradles him to her chest. She tries bouncing. She hums something and I think it's familiar, a riff from a Guns N' Roses song. She spins. Locklin wails and drools all over Gina's leather jacket.

Gina is the only one who'll do this with me. June came once, the day after Locklin was born, then never came back.

"Why does he cry like that?" she wanted to know.

Gina has her nieces and nephews. She's the oldest in her family. She helped raise her sister and three brothers. She knows a little.

"He's just like you," she says, joking, about Locklin. "A total pain in the ass." She lifts him and kisses the back of his red scalp, then hands him to me.

"Thanks," I say, meaning for being here when no one else would be, for being the one and only friend I have at the moment.

"You're welcome," she says. "It's true. You've always been a pain in the ass."

Chapter 73

Two days later, Gina's back in Ohio and Locklin starts throwing up.

I call the doctor's office again. The same nurse says, "Date of birth? He's been here before?"

This time she suggests Pedialyte. She suggests I keep nursing. She says to watch he doesn't become dehydrated. She says to keep checking his tongue and make sure it's moist.

"Try a warm bath. They're soothing," she says.

She says in a perky voice, "Call back and let us know how it's going, Mom."

I bathe Locklin in the sink. He throws up in the water. I see his reflection in the faucet. His eyes are shut. He cries so hard. He's so very small. He's very sick. Dave's at work. I give Locklin Pedialyte. I give him watered-down juice in a dropper, like I would a sick bird. I keep feeding him. He keeps throwing up. I try not to panic. I call the nurse back.

I call back again.

I call back again.

"You might as well bring him in," she says.

It's not colic. It's not a difficult personality. It's not a cold. The doctor who sees us is named Dr. Schott. Any other time, it would have called for a t-shirt, Dr. Schott gives shots, but I don't even see the joke. He says, "We'll call ahead. Go straight to the emergency room. They'll be ready for you."

Locklin has a virus, RSV. Respiratory syntactical virus. It is almost epidemic at Pittsburgh's Children's Hospital this year, Dr. Schott says. The virus' symptoms are a lot like the flu, but in infants, it's serious, even fatal.

I can tell by how quickly the ER doctors see us, by the urgent way the nurses treat my son that he is in danger. On the wall of the examination room, there is a chart, cartoon baby faces in various degrees of distress.

"Because they can't tell us what's wrong," an ER nurse says when she sees me looking at it. I'm looking at it because I'm afraid to look at my son whose cries seem to put him far off the chart.

They put Locklin in a hospital bed that is half crib, half cage. He looks so small, like a bean on a sheet of paper. They give him oxygen through a tiny tube. They put a sensor on his finger. The sensor glows red. It checks his oxygen levels.

"You'll need to watch him," a nurse says. "You want to make sure he doesn't stop breathing."

Locklin has snored since he was born. The day the delivery nurses put him on my belly and he crawled up to nurse, when he curled into me and his starfish hands held on, from the first time he slept outside my body, he snored. And now this is terrifying.

"He probably had the virus before he even left the hospital," the nurse says. "He probably had it all along. Did he cry much?"

Another mother, red-eyed in a man's t-shirt, slippers and sweatpants, who's been here for days with her two-year-old son, Locklin's roommate, says, "You're lucky. I read that a lot of time the really young babies just stop breathing in their sleep."

Chapter 74

Dave has to be back at work. He's slept eight hours in four days. He throws up in the parking lot before and after work, from exhaustion, from worry.

"Go home," I say when he comes in tonight, "you need to rest."

"I can't," he says. "I'll be up all night, worrying."

"We'll be fine," I say.

"Will you be?" he says, and I say, "I'll be fine."

"Can I get you something to eat? Anything?"

He gets me something to eat. He comes back with soup and a flower for me. He puts a teddybear in Locklin's crib. A nurse comes and takes it out.

"Go," I say. "You have to be up for work soon."

He looks ashamed to leave but leaves.

I stay at the hospital with our son. One of the nurses brings in a breast pump. She brings a blanket and pillow and a food tray.

"I didn't know if you'd want this, but there were extras. The brownies almost taste real," she says. She touches my shoulder. She says, "You have to eat to keep your milk up. Try not to worry. We see a lot of this."

She gestures towards Locklin, then out into the rest of the hospital, where all along the hall other children cry. The sound has become like the drone of some sad machinery, because it doesn't stop, not even late at night.

In his caged crib, my son's tiny finger pulses red, the monitor checking his oxygen levels. When he cries, it cuts through everything. He sleeps now. My chair is pulled close.

When I think I'm going to doze off, I put one hand through the steel bars and rest it on his chest to feel the rise and fall of his breathing.

After the nurse leaves, I plug in the pump. It's huge, industrial, double-sided. I turn it on and the vacuum sound is almost soothing. I attach it and the milk pours out of me in long bursts.

The milk is pale, almost purple. My breasts have been so full it hurts to move. Locklin can't nurse. I pump out the milk. I pour it into the plastic containers the nurse has brought and label them with my son's name. She'll come back for them later, take them out on a tray, put them in the refrigerator that's full of other containers just like this, all labeled with the names of so many other mother's children.

Chapter 75

My father used to talk about my hospital stays.

"I'd hate to leave you there at night," he said. "I'd wait until I thought you were asleep, but you'd start screaming as soon as I walked out the door. I could hear you crying all the way to the elevator. The next morning when I'd come, you'd still be crying and calling for me."

My father had to go to work. My mother stayed in the hospital with me. She slept on a cot in her nurse's uniform. She slept next to me, and if I woke up, she was up, too. She brushed and braided my hair. She used a warm washcloth to bathe me when I was in traction and strung up like a puppet. She read to me and watched cartoons and rubbed my head until I'd go to sleep. She got up off the cot in the mornings and went to work on the same floor.

I don't know how any of this was possible. I don't know when she showered. I think my father brought her fresh clothes. I don't know what she ate, if or when. I know my mother believed in the power of medicine. She believed in doctors. But she believed most in her own ability to keep me safe.

"As long as I'm here, nothing will happen to you," she'd say.

It was true and not true.

I loved my mother, but even then, she said, "You better be a good patient and not give anyone trouble." She said, "Don't embarrass me."

I love my mother. I think about calling and telling her what's going on, but I don't.

I love my mother.

I love my mother.

Under my hand, my son's small chest rises and falls.

My mother would know what to do, but she would blame me for not keeping him safe too. If I'd just done things her way, none of this would have happened.

As a child, I'd lie in my hospital bed and scream for my father when my mother was there next to me.

I don't know how that felt, but now I can guess.

Chapter 76

When I do call someone, I call June. Gina's out of town. Elaine doesn't let Dave take calls at the bookstore. I'm scared and think talking to someone might help.

I haven't seen June in weeks, but she'd been there when Locklin was born, so she's the one I call.

I don't know what I expect her to do.

I've been sitting still, watching Locklin breathe. Each time I shift in the chair, I feel my incision. It hasn't fully healed. I still haven't gotten used to my body. It feels collapsed, empty, raw. I still catch myself with my hand on my belly, rubbing the way I did when Locklin was still in there kicking my ribs out.

"I'm just on my way out," June says, "I'll call you later," but she doesn't. She won't. Already my old life is a dock I can't see from this distance.

Locklin's birth was one thing.

What comes later, the actual child, a life, is something else.

Chapter 77

Locklin's pediatrician, the one who asks about the nursery, stops in to see him. After three days, Locklin's doing better and the doctors consider sending him home.

"When was your house built?" the pediatrician wants to know. "You should have your house tested for mold."

Today, his tie is Bugs Bunny and Elmer Fudd. Elmer Fudd points his gun at Bugs, Bugs points a carrot back.

I think about our apartment, its swampy carpet, its drafts and leaks, George's incense floating up through the vents. I look at my son, alert and just starting to nurse again. He cries less. He's getting better. I look at the pediatrician, his wide-open boy face, his spiked gelled hair, and I lie.

I give him details about my mother's house. "It was built in 1973," I say. About the mold testing, I say, "Of course we will."

"We have to move," I tell Dave when he comes in after work.

"Where?" he says. "We have no money."

When Dave bends down into the metal crib to pick up Locklin, Locklin cries.

"Somewhere," I say. "We have to."

Chapter 78

The landlord happily lets us break our lease.

"I'm sure you can find a place that's more suitable to your," she says, pauses, searches for the right word, "needs."

We look at rowhouses on the North Side. They're beautiful, with hardwood floors and stained-glass windows and tiny yards out back, but the neighborhood is rough. There's a porno theater a few blocks over and a halfway house on the same street. A lot of people seem to have pit bulls. The day we're there, a dazed-looking woman zigzags down the middle of the street barefoot. She's thin as a razor. She asks us if we can give her a ride to the hospital because she's pregnant and is ready to have her baby. She asks us for five dollars. Her arms are scratched raw.

We look at another house on the South Side. The basement is unfinished, all dirt. It looks like a cave. Upstairs, there are mouse traps. Dave carries Locklin in his car seat, swings him back and forth to keep him from fussing.

"We'll think about it," I say to the woman after she opens a closet and suggests using it as an extra room for the baby. "A play space," she says, and bends down and tickles Locklin's strapped-in belly. "For the little guy."

The carpet looks ancient. The house smells like mildew. A pipe in the basement leaks, turning the dirt around it to mud. I remember the pediatrician, what he said about mold. The thought of Locklin crawling on the carpet, scurrying around mouse traps, breathing in whatever's in this air, makes me want to weep.

The woman, the owner, says, "You should think fast. This will go soon," and hands us a credit application, which I'm not sure we can pass.

I know we need to live like good parents, responsible people. Our son needs a decent place to live. I'm not sure how we'll afford to do that. Most of the rentals we can afford are like this one, with its basement cave and bad plumbing.

Between Dave and me, we make $60,000 a year, which should be enough, but there are bills, all those credit cards I ran up during my years in New York. There are Dave's student loans.

There's rent and groceries and diapers, car payments, insurance payments, and at the end of every month we're nearly always broke.

"How do you think our credit is?" Dave asks as we walk away and I say, "O.k., I think," then, "I don't know," then, "bad, probably," and Dave, who's been working so much he barely has time to sleep, says, "We're losers," and I say "No, we're not," and Locklin, who Dave's stopped rocking, starts to scream.

When we go back to our car, which is parked a block away on the street, there's something on the windshield. It's a note written on blue stationery.

The note is written in ragged letters, all capitals. It would like to inform us that we've parked in front of a house that is not ours. The owner is old and not well. She has lived here all her life. She needs to keep the spot in front of her house open so the ambulance will have a place to park when it comes for her.

FIND YOUR OWN DAMN PLACE, it says, then GOD BLESS.

Chapter 79

My cousin's ex-wife is renting out a condominium in Trafford, a quarter mile from my mother's house. "At least come and see it before you turn your nose up," my mother says.

The condominium's reasonable, $500 a month. It's clean, with two big bedrooms, three floors, and a deck off the back. There's no deposit, no credit check. "That's what family is," my mother says, as if she's trying to translate Greek for me.

Of course she wants us here. Living here would add an hour to Dave's commute. It would put me within kicking distance. But I would be close by if her health got worse. I'd be closer to my campus job. She'd be close by for Locklin.

If I'd once thought of the apartment in the city as a floating life raft, this would be more like a dingy strapped to the mother ship.

"I'm trying to keep an open mind," I say to Dave, who says, "It's not like we have a ton of options." The skin around his eyes is cracked and bleeding. There are paper cuts on his hands that won't heal. Some nights, he doesn't sleep, so he tries to write with Locklin on his lap.

"Your commute will suck," I say, and he says, "It would be nice to have a place to park." I say, "I grew up here," not like it's a good thing, and he says, "I like yard work. I think I could like yard work."

We go see the condo. It's cream-colored. There are shrubs and lilies in front. There's a driveway and a garage, a pool and a basketball court. There's no mold. Inside, the walls are painted beautiful colors, a combination of deep tones and muted pastels. The colors remind me of the desert, of Santa Fe, peaceful. When my cousin's ex-wife remarried, she married an artist. The master bedroom is the color of a Dreamsicle, a rich pure orange.

"We've loved it here," Tawny, my cousin's ex-wife, says. "We're sad to be moving, but we're running out of room."

The space is packed with furniture, huge pieces that would fit better in a concert hall. There is a floor-to-ceiling China cabinet and an entertainment system on one wall, and an overstuffed sectional sofa that wraps around the other walls. There's a massive dining room set, and two huge arm chairs, and upstairs, a bed runs the full width of one bedroom. The only way to get on or off the bed is to climb up from the bottom.

It could be all this furniture that is making me feel like the walls are closing in, the way walls do in fun houses. It's hard to breathe.

It doesn't help that one of Tawny's kids, Aunt Thelma's granddaughter, a little girl with a caramel tan and macramé ankle bracelets above each of her chubby feet, keeps climbing me.

"What you name?" she keeps saying. "What you doing here?" When I sit down on the sofa, she works her way up to my shoulders, puts her arms around my neck, and bites the back of my head.

"Marissa," Tawny yells. "No biting."

Marissa grabs my neck with her round little hands and tries to strangle me.

Tawny says, "Knock it off," and just like that Marissa lets go, scampers across the sofa like a squirrel and plops down in Tawny's lap. She stares at me, hard. It feels like a challenge. "What you doing here?" she says again, and Tawny puts a hand gently over her mouth.

"You'll like it here, too," Tawny says. "You'll be close to your mom."

I can tell by Marissa's eyes that, underneath Tawny's hand, she's smirking. The girl doesn't seem to blink. She seems older than she is, like she knows something, like she's not a little girl at all. Tawny takes her hand away, and Marissa sticks out her tongue.

Whatever she knows, she's not telling.

Chapter 80

Off the back deck of the condo, there are woods and a stream. It's quiet. Locklin is in his crib, sleeping. This place, without all the city sounds, seems to suit him. There aren't many street lights, but there are stars, too many to count. There are crickets and, somewhere, there's an owl. There's parking. There's yard work.

Dave and I are sit on the deck. It's Spring, still cool. I'm on extended maternity leave and haven't gone back to work yet. Dave's commute is, as we knew it would be, terrible and Elaine is worse, but we're working on a way he'll be able to quit and stay home with Locklin in the fall. We're trying hard to save money, but a baby's expensive.

"It's just temporary," Dave says about the bookstore. He doesn't complain, even though he could. I try not to complain.

Together, we're working on something more permanent. We both write when we can. We come out to the deck to read or just sit and talk. The air smells like
wet grass. It smells like it did when I was a child. The stars look the same, too. Very little has changed. There's comfort in that.

"I used to play in these woods," I tell Dave, who grew up not far away himself. Before his parents moved to Michigan, they lived in Irwin.

Irwin is also in Westmoreland County. Westmoreland County, where Dave and I lived before and live now, is known for a few things, but especially supernatural things, things like UFOs and Bigfoot. Westmoreland County is home to Stan Gordon, the world's #1 Bigfoot expert. It's home to an annual international UFO Convention, often held at Seton Hill University. Seton Hill is a Catholic University, a lot like the one I went to in Erie, where Gina and I took that parapsychology course years ago.

There's something about people around here, their love of supernatural things, that fascinates me, but I can't understand it. So many people in one place, wanting to believe in things other people think are impossible.

It's easy to dismiss lives as small, whatever they are. I'm trying to learn to do the opposite.

"Did you ever think you'd end up back here?" Aunt Thelma says when she comes to check out our new place. She brings housewarming gifts – wash cloths, napkins and paper towels. "I mean, look at you. A wife, a mother. Did you ever imagine? Can you believe this?"

Since we moved here, my mother has seemed almost happy. I check in on her every day. She drives down in her red car, her Ray Bans on, to check in on her grandson. Dave goes to her house on the weekends to cut her grass. We have dinner together, all four of us, most Sundays, whenever Elaine doesn't call Dave in to work on his day off.

I don't believe in transformations, but my mother, maybe because she feels more a part of things, maybe because she feels safer with us nearby, seems transformed. Maybe I am, too, a little.

Today I find a huge pillar of toilet paper stuffed into our doorway, along with a jumbo pack of diapers and t-shirts for Locklin.

"It's nothing," my mother says when I call to ask. "I had coupons. They were on sale."

She says, "Is Dave off tomorrow?"

She says, "I'll watch Locklin for a few hours to give you two a break."

"Isn't life funny?" Aunt Thelma says. "Well what do you think about that?"

Later this year, Jane Goodall, renowned expert on primates, will go on NPR and say she believes in Bigfoot.
She'll cite Native American lore, images on ancient totems, mysterious hair samples, cross-cultural sightings in North America, China, Brazil and the Netherlands.

"Without a doubt, he exists," she'll say.

It will be a call-in show, and one listener will want to know what she's trying to prove. He'll want to know how, as a scientist, as a rational person, she could be serious.

"I believe," she'll say, "because I want to believe."

Chapter 81

When I come to pick up Locklin, my mother has him outside in his stroller. It's late June. The sun shines and my mother wears her Ray Bans. Locklin wears sunglasses, too, little red heart-shaped ones, and an outfit my mother has gotten him from J.C. Penney's.

My mother and I have an agreement. Whenever she watches Locklin, she can make at least some of the rules. This means she gets to dress him in ridiculous get-ups and parade him around like a piñata. Sometimes she dresses him like an accountant, with a miniature clip-on tie, plaid suspenders and cuffed pants. Sometimes, she goes for a seasonal theme – like the orange sweatsuit with the green fringed beanie that makes him look like a carrot. "For Spring, for Easter," my mother says.

Today, it's a fuzzy yellow romper – a sunsuit, my mother calls it. There is a coordinating hat with a beak for a brim.

"What does a duckie say?" my mother coos into Locklin's stroller. "What do you call a bad doctor?"

Locklin, who will say his first words -- "duck" and "light" -- in only a few more weeks, is still just on the verge of speech. Language gives people a sense of control over their lives. This is something I think my son knew almost from the start. Right now, powerless, he's still mostly red fists and spread toes. He punches and kicks and looks outraged. My mother, in her sunglasses and floppy pink sunhat, looks like she expects the paparazzi to show up.

"What's the big deal?" she says. "The neighbors like to see him dressed nice."

She reaches for Locklin's fists, which she lifts over his head again and again, like he's doing the wave. There are wings sewn into the romper, little flaps that connect the arms to the body.

"Doesn't he look smart?' she says. "Doesn't he look just adorable?" She lets go of his arms. Locklin takes a swing. "You caught us," she says. "We were about to do our rounds."

The pacifier my mother is always trying to jam into my son's mouth is on the driveway. The beak hat is farther away, in the grass. I suspect he's launched both of them out of the stroller. I suspect there's been a fight.

They are, my mother and son, at six months and 71 years, profoundly dysfunctional. My mother, so used to bullying, has finally found someone she can't control. And she loves him for it.

"You shouldn't dress him like that," I say. "It's undignified. It'll take years of therapy to undo."

"I just hope I'm around to see it," she says, and bends down, lovingly, right into Locklin's strike zone.

Chapter 82

My mother's taken to saying things like this. Her comments are often out of context, out of place. I don't understand what's happening.

We're coming back from another doctor's visit. She's gotten a good report, and now she's quiet, staring out the passenger side window. I'm trying to concentrate on driving, but it's hard. Lately, my brain is filled up with the sounds of baby toys and crying and kiddie videos starring dinosaurs and chipmunks whose voices sound loaded with helium.

"Tickle Me Elmo" is going at it in the back seat. Locklin punches Elmo in the gut. Elmo squeals. Over and over. That tickles. That tickles. I'm thinking about things like brakes and turn signals and so I don't notice at first how quiet my mother is until she leans over and puts a hand on my arm. She says, "I just want five more years." She says, "I have a lot of life in me."

I think she is being her usual dramatic self and so I say, "Let's go for 10," and then, when she doesn't speak, I say, "Stop that. You're fine."

She does seem fine. Never, in recent memory, has she seemed so young. When she parades Locklin around the neighborhood, she comes close to skipping. "You're a little bit of a miracle," the doctor said to my mother, and my mother said, "What do you expect? I have a grandson to think about."

My mother lets go of my arm and I glance over, but her face is turned away. We drive through downtown Trafford.

Outside there's the park where her father died. That was 1964, the year I was born, a year before my parents adopted me.

"My dad would have loved you," my mother says, and I think I would have loved him, an orphan like me, with his dark eyes and skinny legs, his suspenders and fedoras. "He would have really loved this one," she says about Locklin, and Elmo giggles.

"You're fine," I say to my mother again, and Locklin, from the back seat tries to say the word, too.

Chapter 83

Here is my mother, dressed up in a puffy-paint "World's Greatest Grandma" sweatshirt she bought herself.

Here she is in her kitchen, dancing from sink to countertop, polkas blaring on the radio.

Here is my son, tucked into a highchair my mother snagged at a yard sale, baby cereal smeared like war paint across his face. Here is my mother laughing, not worried about the mess.

"He's a good little eater," she says.

She says, "I wish your father were alive to see him."

She says, "He looks just like you."

"I love you," my mother says to my son. She wipes his face, pops him out of the highchair and cuddles him until he kicks himself loose. Locklin thrashes and wails for his freedom, my son, who looks just like me.

"I love you," my mother says. "You don't even know how much."

Chapter 84

Three years from now, my son, with all the power of language, will say, "My old grandma was the best friend I ever had."

Chapter 85

My mother will live for two more years, not the five she hoped for, not the 10 I joked about and expected.

The cancer we'd almost forgotten, with all the focus on her heart, has come back and spread. The doctors are still optimistic. It means more surgery, a lumpectomy, maybe more, they won't know for sure until they go in.

The nurse who preps my mother for surgery is kind. She wears clogs and a smock with balloons and clouds and rainbows all over it. Her hair is pulled into a high ponytail. Overhead, the TV is tuned to "Good Morning America."

"I like your uniform," my mother says, her voice already thick, groggy. "You know, I used to be a nurse."

"We make the worst patients, you know," the nurse says as she undoes my mother's hospital robe. "You're not going to give me any trouble, are you?"

"Not me," my mother says, half smiling.

The nurse lifts my mother's right arm, then her breast out of the robe. The breast lolls to the side, soft and white against blue cotton, like a cloud but heavy, full of rain. The skin is stretched thin and I can see the veins underneath. The areola is large and brown and I remember the times when I was young and first saw my mother naked, how astonishing it was, how I couldn't imagine ever being like her. In the shower, her breasts would hang nearly to her waist. Later, when she'd get dressed, she'd have to bend over and lift them into huge pointy cups, first one breast then the other. She'd snap the bra closed, four hook-and-eye clasps, before she'd stand up.

Since those days, I've bathed my mother. I've dressed her. I know her body almost the way I know my son's.

"Be happy," my mother would say when I was almost a teenager, with band-aid x's on my chest. "You'll never have to carry all this weight around."

The nurse marks my mother's breast with a series of small x's. "We have to show the doctor where to cut," she explains. The marks look like stops on a road map. They look like intersections. The nurse uses a purple marker. On the out-side of the marker, there is a ruler and an ad from a pharmaceutical company.

"Here," the nurse says, and snaps the cap on the marker, then hands it to me. "You might as well keep it. We can only use them once."

My mother, moving in and out of consciousness, before the nurse wheels her away, leans her head to me. "Heart

of my heart," she says, as she's always said, and I hold onto her hand before the doors to surgery snap open and I have to let go.

I put the purple marker in my purse. Weeks later, I'll use it to grade student essays. I'll write things in the margins, like "comma splice" and "cut." I'll write "fragment" and "more." I'll write, "What are you afraid to say?"

Chapter 86

The first few weeks in the hospital, my mother seems to be getting better. She wants Locklin to come and see her. I'm afraid he'll be afraid of all the tubes and wires. I'm afraid he might, just by being in a hospital again, get sick.

"You need to let him come," Aunt Thelma says. "She'll be home soon," I say, and Aunt Thelma says, "I think you need to bring him now."

They are good together, my mother and son, who, at two, already knows how to comfort people. He lets my mother wear his baseball hat. My mother cocks it on top of her head, backwards, b-boy style, and Locklin curls up on the hospital bed next to her to share her dinner.

They fight over the coffee. She saves him the pudding. The nurses draw faces on surgical gloves, then blow them up and give them to my son. He makes my mother hold one and he holds another one. They do puppet shows. They make their gloves howl like wolves at the moon.

My mother wants to know what I'm making for dinner. She asks every day and whatever I say she says, "That sounds good." I sneak her food – meatballs, strawberries, tomatoes from her garden. I bring her soup and milkshakes. She seems stronger. Then one day, when I get to the hospital, there's a triage cart outside her door. She's begun throwing up and can't stop.

"I'm not up for it," she says later when I ask if she wants me to bring Locklin in. "Give him a kiss for me."

So many people come and see her. She asks me to make them stop, but I can't. My mother says she's tired. I tell her she'll be o.k., it will just take time. She says, "This time it's too much."

She asks again, no more visitors, and for the first time I say what we both know.

"You have to give people a chance to say goodbye," I say.

My mother tries to nod, but her head is too heavy to lift off the pillow.

Chapter 87

When my mother dies, she dies at home, in her own bed. During her last week in the hospital, she stops taking her pain medication. She convinces the doctors and nurses she feels better. They convince me, or I wanted them to convince me, that she is doing well. Then she can't sit up in the car on the way home and cries as we work to get her out of the car, the pain is that bad.

When I call for a hospice nurse to come and check in on her, the doctors seem puzzled.

"She's not dying," one says to me. "She needs rehab and time, but she'll be okay."

Home now, she wants to sit in her chair. She wants to watch *Gone With The Wind*. She is angry. She wants a fight.

"You've always had a nervous laugh," she says to Aunt Thelma, who laughs and sounds nervous.

"I see you're still in diapers," she says to Locklin, who looks down to check.

"Stop telling me what the hell to do," she says to me. "You're not my mother."

When I ask her if we've all done something, when I ask why she's so angry, her voice comes back down, like a bird settling. "Of course not, honey," she says. "I'm sorry."

She refuses to take her medications. She refuses to see the woman from rehab who shows up to teach her exercises. She wants to talk things out until she can't talk any more. She says a lot of things. She says she's happy to see me settled.

"For a while I thought you'd never get there," she says and tries to pat my hand. Her skin is like gauze.

"I'm not that settled," I say. "I still need you around."

"Yes you are," she says. "No you don't."

She loves Dave. She wishes she had more time. She wants us to keep the house. She wants us not to sell it, but she'll understand if we do.

"Whatever you do, keep the dining room set," she says. "It's good. I fought your father like crazy to get it."

She says to remember to pay my taxes. "Save a little each month," she says. "Put it in an envelope marked Taxes. Don't blow it."

"And bake every once in a while," she says. "It won't kill you."

As for Locklin, she says, "Make sure he remembers me."

Chapter 88

There are pictures of my mother everywhere in our house, her house. At Christmas, I work my way through her old recipe boxes and bake a little. I give Aunt Thelma the dining room set because she can appreciate it and because all that glass and heavy wood makes me nervous, first with Locklin and then Phelan, my daughter.

I was pregnant when my mother died, but I didn't know it yet. My mother would have loved that I had a girl.

"One of each," she'd say. "Like you planned it that way."

It took a long time for the engravers to come and add my mother's name to the tombstone she shares with my father in the cemetery in Braddock. For a while, I tried to pretend she wasn't dead. Before we moved into her house, I'd leave lights on. I'd drive by on my way back from campus and see the lights and think she was home, watching TV, working on a new afghan. I'd think I should stop and check on things. When I'd go to her grave and her name wasn't there, it was the same thing. Like it wasn't finished. And then one day her name was there, and it still wasn't finished.

As for Locklin remembering her, my mother didn't need to worry. Sometimes he and his sister still play with an old phone I keep in my office in the basement.

The phone belonged to my grandmother. My mother kept it after my grandmother died and I keep it now. It's black and heavy. It has a dial and a paper circle in the center of the dial with my grandmother's old phone number on it.

My grandmother's house, Aunt Thelma's house now, is a mile away, in downtown Trafford. When my grandmother was alive, she and my mother would talk every day.

"She drives me crazy," my mother would say, and then, because she'd forgotten an ingredient in a recipe or saw something on TV, my mother would dial her mother. My grandmother would answer and say, "Where've you been?"

My daughter, Phelan, is one. She doesn't talk much. When they play, Locklin controls the conversation. This is how he likes it, and she doesn't mind as long as he lets her flick the dial every once in a while. Sometimes he calls Luke Skywalker or The Hulk, but often he talks to my mother who, according to my son, lives in the sky.

Sometimes he'll come and get me to play, too.

"My old grandma," he'll say. "She wants to talk to you." He'll say, "My old grandma's on the phone. Boy are you going to get it."

Sometimes I pick up.

I say, "Hi mom." I say, "Where've you been?"

I say, "Locklin's good. He misses you."

I say, "This skirt does not make me look fat."

I say, "I love you, too."

I say, "Goodbye."

Epilogue

Years later, I'm in the kitchen. Phelan is four. While I mix dough, she sneaks into the dining room and opens a bag of flour the size of a ham. I don't know this. I should. I hear her yell, "Snow, snow, snow!" I hear, "Winter!"

I look out the window as the mixer whirs away. Whenever I bake, I think about my mother. The day is sunny, snowflake-free. Phelan still shouts from the other room. There's a space between the time I hear something and the moment I figure out what it means.

Flour is everywhere – in her hair, in the stereo, in her shoes. Later I'll find flour in her underwear and flour in her socks. But right now, she smiles up at me, flour stuck like snowflakes – exactly like snowflakes – in her eyelashes, flour smudged on her pink cheeks, flour caught in the blonde pigtails that stick out like antennae.

"Look at me," she says. "I'm baking."

Locklin is seven now and in charge of the dough.

Every year around the holidays, Dave, who hates chaos, flees the house, and the kids and I make a lovely mess.

Growing up, I didn't get to bake with my mother. It made her nervous. "I don't like people in my kitchen," she'd say as she anchored a childproof gate between the kitchen and dining room. "To keep the dog out," she'd say.

I know now that my mother loved the solitary time baking gave her. It offered an excuse to detach from the rest of the world, from my father and me, from the dog, and make something her own. It's what I do when I write, when I close my office door and leave my children and husband on the other side. "A room of one's own," Virginia Woolf called it.

It wasn't until after Locklin was born that my mother finally gave over and decided to teach me to bake. Our first lesson, bread, was a disaster. My mother told me to show up at 5 a.m. I was late, 5:15, and looked a mess. My mother wasn't happy. Her gray hair was curled. She had on her favorite track suit, purple velour with gold piping at the cuffs. She wore tennis shoes. She looked like she'd been waiting a long time.

"What's the matter with you?" she said. "You have to start bread early."

I didn't know what that meant.

I didn't know what she meant when she said, "Bread is serious business. Bread is no joke," and whacked me on the arm with her wooden spoon.

"Look," she said when I buried my forearms in the bowl of sticky dough and waddled them around. "Do you want to learn or not?"

She picked up her own bowl of dough and pulled it to her belly like a child. She dipped one arm in and lifted the dough up and over, whipping more than kneading, the muscles in her arm flexed and solid and nowhere near old.

"This is how you do it," she said. "You have to work it. You have to mean it."

My mother talked about yeast and bread as living things – things to conquer, things you could kill if you weren't careful. She didn't use measuring cups and spoons. "You just know," she said, her hands measuring flour and sugar by weight, by how the powders moved through her fingers. "You can feel it."

She's been dead for five years now. I still feel the weight of that.

"You need to learn how to do this," she said. "Because when I die, then what?"

In the dining room, my daughter spreads more flour on the table. My son holds a rolling pin. We laugh and smooth out the mounds until there's just a dusting.

I separate the dough into bowls, one for each of us. My son rolls his into tiny balls. He launches them like cannonballs with his thumb.

Within a few hours, the house will fill with smells I remember from childhood, and I'll lay the golden loaves onto racks to cool.

"Look," Phelan will say when her father comes home, as she takes him by the hand to show him what we've made. "Isn't it beautiful?"

About the Author

Lori Jakiela is the author of the memoir, *Miss New York Has Everything* (Warner/Hatchette, 2006), and a poetry collection – *Spot the Terrorist!*(Turning Point, 2012). Her work has been published in *The New York Times, The Washington Post, The Chicago Tribune, The Pittsburgh Post-Gazette* and more. She is a recipient of the City of Asylum-Pittsburgh Prize, a Golden Quill Award from the Press Club of Western Pennsylvania, and has been nominated for the Pushcart Prize many times. She teaches in the writing programs at The University of Pittsburgh-Greensburg and Chatham University, and lives outside of Pittsburgh with her husband, the writer Dave Newman, and their children. Her third memoir – *Belief Is Its Own Kind of Truth, Maybe* – will be published by Atticus Books in Summer 2015. For more, visit http://lorijakiela.net.